Going to the

C000111118

A Guide to British First Cl

By Robin Osmond and Peter David Lush

Checking the score at Leicester (PDL)

Going to the Cricket
Errata and update slip

Middlesex CCC Website: middlesexccc.com
p.46: Lancashire's Web site is lccc.co.uk
p.82: Warwickshire's postcode is B5 7QU
p.92: Yorkshire club shop is now 0113-274-0460
Our apologies!

TIONS Ltd.

Going to the Cricket

A Guide to British First Class Cricket Grounds

A CIP catalogue record for this book is available from the British Library.

First published in Great Britain in April 1999 by:
London League Publications Ltd.
P.O. Box 10441, London E14 0SB

ISBN: 0-9526064-7-X

Cover design by: Stephen McCarthy Graphic Design
                          46, Clarence Road London N15 5BB

Printed and bound by: Catford Print Centre, PO Box 563, Catford,
                          London SE6 4PY

About the Authors

Robin Osmond:
Formerly a Director of Social Services and independent Social Services Consultant who would like to see the word 'retirement' deleted from common usage. A life long follower of Middlesex and Arsenal as a member of the MCC and Gloucestershire he is delighted at the decision to admit women to membership and believes that the old Jessop Tavern pessimists should take great encouragement from last season's magnificent match against Surrey at Cheltenham..

Robin is much involved in developing junior cricket at Hawkesbury Cricket Club, a very occasional slow left arm bowler, part time cricket writer and a photographer whose interests range from black and white printing to digital imaging.. He is an enthusiastic e-mailer who would welcome messages or comments about the book or anything else on: osmond@hawkesbury.u-net.com

Peter David Lush:
Is not a former TCCB official and England tour manager! (And is making rare use of his middle name to avoid unnecessary confusion). A Londoner, played for King Alfred School first XI - which was very short of players. Retired from playing Cricket at 16 after seeing Mike and Steve Gatting play at Brondesbury CC (in their younger days), and realising how far he was from reaching a reasonable standard. Made a comeback in his mid 30s to play for Malvern CC in east London, once taking five wickets, before finally retiring from active Cricket in 1989.

A Middlesex member, his main sporting interests apart from Cricket are Football (West Ham United) and Rugby League (London Broncos). Has co-written or edited three Rugby League books with Dave Farrar. When not researching sports books, and taking photos of sports grounds, he works as a freelance housing and personnel consultant.

Robin Osmond and Peter David Lush, with Dave Farrar, were the authors of "*From Arundel to Zimbabwe*", London League Publications' first cricket guide.

Thank You
We would like to thank all the club officials, tourist information and travel centre staff who provided information for the book. Dave Farrar worked hard checking information and using the internet. Sandra's proof-reading and advice on tourism were greatly appreciated, as was Amanda's hospitality and support. Toni checked travel and other information rigorously. Mike Berry provided information on Minor Counties cricket. We would also like to thank all the advertisers and people who subscribed to the book in advance.

Preface

From Arundel to Zimbabwe, our first guide to cricket grounds was published in April 1997 and with the wide interest and importance of the World Cup in England we decided to pursue the idea of a new guide in 1999. However, *Going to the Cricket* concentrates on the eighteen principal county grounds and includes the two Oxbridge grounds, Edinburgh, Dublin and Amstelveen.

Although it is primarily a factual guide, it includes brief historical information about some of the great players and county achievements on the Test and county grounds which have contributed to their unique characteristics. The comments on ground facilities reflect our personal observations, and while some are more complimentary than others, we believe they are fair comments on the current position. Most of the eighteen county grounds began life in the nineteenth century and are bound to have prospered, struggled to maintain the status quo or in some cases the county is considering whether to stay or move.

On the whole there are encouraging signs in refurbishment, new building and other improvements around the grounds. What has not changed at all are the differences in standards and facilities for county members and the general public. For anyone consigned to the popular side, there is no comparison with the comforts and enjoyment of the members' areas and the corporate hospitality boxes and marquees. These are the priorities which determine who gets the best seats for all forms of cricket and the rest have to take their chance. This includes the risk of sitting next to a crowd of hooligans; although this problem is not exclusive to the popular side. The key issue is how to ensure that ordinary cricket followers, with young families, on modest incomes can be assured of good standards and trouble free days at the cricket.

Gloucestershire, Glamorgan, Somerset and Worcestershire have extended their reciprocal arrangements for members to include free admission for championship matches against the other fourteen counties. This is a positive move which could easily be extended within other neighbouring counties in London, the Midlands and the North of England.

Pavilions and club restaurants provide much better quality and choice of food and refreshments than the dull fare in the kiosks around the ground. Apart from big match occasions on the Test Match grounds standards are well behind what is generally available in public houses or in motorway service areas. It has been suggested that people don't really care, but there must be opportunities for local suppliers and catering businesses to do better than hamburgers, jacket potatoes and flavourless sandwiches. Would it not be possible to open up the use of members' areas including the catering facilities to anyone who has paid the entrance fee for a championship match?

Many counties offer free or reduced admission prices for disabled and visually impaired people and in some cases for their carers. Some have improved facilities and Durham have shown what can be done through positive attitudes and designated seating at the Riverside Stadium. The ultimate aim must be for counties to provide wheelchair spaces in seating areas to enable wheelchair users and their carers to sit in the crowd.

We have included some information about scoreboards which are so often a source of interest and amusement and, in some circumstances, neither understandable or visible. A number of grounds have museums which are well worth visiting although they are not all always open on match days and more information could be provided about them. Club shops are often basically merchandising outlets for cricket clothing with county logos and cricket equipment, and it would be nice to see more new and second hand cricket book sections.

World Cup matches on grounds all over the country will provide testing challenges and exciting opportunities for county authorities and spectators who have become accustomed to the idea that big cricketing occasions are reserved for the Test Match grounds. If things go well, there is no reason why international games should not feature at a number of county grounds.

We received a number of helpful comments about *From Arundel to Zimbabwe* and would like more, particularly about those aspects which are best known to those who regularly attend their local grounds.

Robin Osmond
March 1999

Cricket Grounds Quiz

1. Which County once played a fixture at Margam?
2. On which two grounds did a bowler achieve a hat trick with LBW decisions and who were the bowlers concerned ?
3. Which five Gloucestershire players have scored a double century at Cheltenham ?
4. Which famous soldier was born at St. Marks Vicarage by The Oval ?
5. On which ground did Frank Chester stand in his first county match ?
6. On which ground did Tony Lewis take 3 for 18 having not previously bowled in first class cricket for four years?
7. On which famous ground was the pavilion used for a hospital centre during the first World War?
8. On which ground did WG Grace score the first recorded triple century?
9. Where did a Gloucestershire bowler achieve a hat-trick of stumpings?
10. On which ground did A.E. Fagg achieve the unique feat of scoring a double century in each innings of a match?
11. On which ground did Hobbs complete his 126th Century?
12. Where did Brian Lara score 375 to break the world Test record?
13. Which county ground was previously known as the Racecourse Ground?
14. On which county ground did P.G.H. Fender score a century in 25 minutes?
15. Which ground is known as The Basin Reserve?
16. On which ground did the Australians once make 721 runs in a day?
17. On which ground is there a lime tree within the field of play?
18. Which famous cricketer was the son of the vicar of Bognor Regis and on which ground did he make his debut?
19. On which ground did Somerset play their first 'home game' outside the County boundary ?
20. Which County plays at Ynysangharad Park ?
21. Which ground is overlooked by the twisted spire of the parish church?
22. Which ground is known as the Castle Park Ground?
23. On which ground did Sir Garfield Sobers score 365 and break Sir Leonard Hutton's record at the time ?
24. On which ground did Harold Gimblett score 120 in 80 minutes on his debut for Somerset?
25. Which ground is known as Pen-y-Pound ?

26. Which ground is known as May's Bounty ?
27. Who played cricket on Gosden Common on July 26 1745?
28. Who founded Trent Bridge?
29. Which county played at Acklam Park and where is it ?
30. On which ground did Hedley Verity take 10 wickets for 10 runs?
31. On which ground was the first Test Match between England and Australia played?
32. On which ground did Gilbert Jessop hit a six into the railway station?
33. On which ground did Ashdown, Woolley, Ames and Watt score 219 runs in 71 minutes to defeat Gloucestershire?
34. Which famous author took 7 for 99 in a match at Lord's in 1899?
35. Which 'services' ground is the only one still used for county cricket?
36. Which County once played county games on the Wagon Works ground?
37. Which county ground is closest to the sea ?
38. Name five rivers that adjoin first class county cricket grounds
39. Name the famous club ground that featured a county championship game for the first time in 1998
40. Which four counties will play all their home championship matches at the county ground in 1999?
41. Which grounds are otherwise known as Southchurch Park, The Mote, and The Gnoll?
42. Where would you find the following Ends ? Diglis Road; Cathedral Road; Vauxhall; Nackington Road and Kirkstall Lane
43. On which ground did M.J. Stewart catch seven in one innings?
44. On which ground did a Test Match end in a tie ?
45. Name four grounds on which Kent no longer play county cricket?
46. On which ground did Denis Compton score his 18th and record breaking century in 1947?
47. Where would you find the Bridge of Sighs on a cricket ground ?
48. In which country is the Test Match ground known as Bourda found?
49. Where did Jim Laker take his record haul of 19 wickets in a Test Match?
50. On which ground did Anil Kumble become the second man in Test history to take all ten wickets in an innings ?

(Answers on page 133)

The Cricket Society

Offers:

- Publications - biannual journal and news bulletin eight times a year
- Monthly meetings addressed by prominent cricket personalities, held in Bath, Birmingham, Durham and London
- Top class Dinners
- Comprehensive cricket library
- Annual coaching scholarships for youngsters and Kwik Cricket schools competition
- Cricket Society playing XI
- Cricketers Service held annually at St Johns Wood Church, London
- Annual awards presented for outstanding play and for the best cricket publication

Whether you want to play the game, talk about it, watch it, read about it, write about it, encourage it..The Cricket Society has something for you all for 25p a week!

Annual Subscriptions:	*Joining between July & 31 October*
Full £13	£6.50
Senior Citizen £9	£4.50
Junior £9	£4.50
Family £18.50	£9.25

For further information or details of how you can join over 2,000 existing members around the World, please contact:
Eric Budd, Honorary Secretary,
16, Storey Court
39, St John's Wood Road
London NW8 8QX
Tel: 0171-820-1866 (Work) or 0171-286-7054 (home)

How to use this book

Road travel: We recommend using a standard road map with this book. The sketch maps are not drawn to scale, and only cover areas by the grounds.

Facilities: The facilities provided by the counties at the permanent first class grounds vary depending on the match and crowd expected. If a particular facility is important for you, we would recommend checking in advance.

Facilities for people with disabilities: Many counties have flexible policies on reduced admission, depending on the match, crowd expected etc. Some facilities need to be booked in advance. We would recommend phoning in advance to check - especially if visiting a ground for the first time.

Membership: Information can be obtained from the County directly. We have not included it in this book as the rates become out of date. Full membership usually provides for free ground admission, except for National Westminster Trophy and Benson & Hedges knockout rounds, use of the pavilion and all members' facilities at the County's home grounds for all matches. There are also reciprocal arrangements for use of members' facilities when the member's County are playing away, subject to availability, and after paying the ground admission fee.

Rapid Cricketline numbers and other information lines: Calls charged at premium rates.

There are bound to be mistakes in the book. We have visited every first class ground in England and Wales, but there can be changes that we are not aware of at the time of production. Please let us know any mistakes you find, so that we can make corrections in the future. Please send comments or corrections to: London League Publications Ltd, P.O. Box 10441, London E14 0SB.

Please note that the authors and London League Publications Ltd do not accept any liability for any loss, injury or inconvenience sustained by people as a result of using the information or advice in this book.

Contents

Permanent first class grounds

The pavilion clock at Grange Cricket Club, Edinburgh (PDL)

MCC and Middlesex
Lord's

Address: Lord's Ground, St. John's Wood Road, London, NW8 8QN
Capacity: 29,500
Telephone numbers:

MCC:
Secretariat: 0171-289-1611   **Fax:** 0171-289-9100
Ticket Enquiries: 0171-289-8979   **Fax:** 0171-266-3459
Prospects of play: 0171-286-8011
Lord's Shop: 0171-432-1021   **Fax:** 0171-432-1007
Gestetner Tours of Lords: 0171-432-1033 **Fax:** 0171-266-3825
Indoor school: 0171-432-1014/5   **Fax:** 0171-432-1060
Library: 0171-289-1611   **Fax:** 0171-432-1062
Web site: www.lords.org

Middlesex CCC:
0171-289-1300   **Fax:** 0171-289-5831
Membership: 0171-286-5453   **Shop:** 0171-286-1310
Clubcall: 0891-525137
Cricket & squash centre (Finchley): 0181-346-8020

Description and Historical Comment:
Lord's is a special place intensely private and public, whether on your own or bumping into friends it encapsulates the magic of cricket. The first game was on 22 June 1814 when MCC beat Hertfordshire by an innings and 27 runs. The old pavilion burnt down in July 1825, was replaced in time for the following season, while the present one, designed by Frank V. Verity, opened in 1890. Lord's has always changed, yet enough remains for continuity and for it to seem the same in an enigmatic combination of ancient and very modern buildings offset with trees and garden areas.
Some yearn for the old Mound and even more for the Tavern concourse and recall the days of childhood dreams when you sat on the grass or had a picnic at the Nursery End. Memories of Sir Donald Bradman and Compton,

Lindwall and Miller, Sir Gary Sobers, Hall and Griffiths adorning the square and England making a fight of it and occasionally winning Test Matches.

Middlesex, founded in 1864, accepted an invitation from MCC in 1876 to play at Lord's and have been there ever since. Middlesex were traditionally the county of amateurs with the Fords, Studds, and Lyttletons and Stoddart who captained England, and Plum Warner who led the team to their second championship in 1921 in his famous last match against Surrey. Patsy Hendren and Jack Hearne were the prolific run scorers between the wars before the unforgettable Compton and Edrich soon afterwards. The Brearley and Gatting years in the 1980s and 1990s brought consistent championship and cup successes and in the 1996 Wisden, Engel and Bailey concluded that Middlesex were just the top side in fifty years of championship cricket since the war.

Still too snooty for some, Lord's has moved with the times and the pavilion is thankfully no longer the last bastion of male chauvinism and privilege. More ladies will enlighten the "golf club" masculinity of hospitality boxes and in house catering might offer fish as well as roast beef as the dish of the day. For the general public the problem is how to get into the big occasions because of the cost of tickets and the difficulty of getting them. This is not only a problem for Lord's, but why not have a small allocation available on the day with the emphasis on families and young people?

The space capsule shaped Nat West Media Centre bridges the Compton and Edrich Stand and much noise and hammer bashing resounded across the ground in 1998. An elegant and futuristic design, ideal for the media on big occasions but how does it justify its existence for the rest of the year? The replay screen is welcome and there is good signage around the ground.

Views from the Boundary:
Members' areas: *Pavilion, Warner stand, Allen stand, Tavern upper & concourse.*

MCC have described Lord's as a series of pavilions each one reflecting the age in which it was built in the context of the ground as a whole. The replacement of the old Grandstand means that, apart from a few places at the bottom of the Compton and Edrich stands, there are good views from all over the ground. Best at the top of the pavilion: behind the bowlers arm, quiet, near a bar and a bird's eye view of the ground. It is sociable in the Warner; affable but more inhibited above the old Tavern; companionable and clubbish in the Allen Stand mainly because it's members only and hard to find over the Bridge of Sighs. In the exotic Michael Hopkins Mound Stand the views are outstanding but the ambience at the top level is uncompromisingly corporate. Nicholas Grimshaw's beautifully designed Grandstand (1998) has its own 180 seater restaurant with viewing on two levels that sandwich a row of glass fronted hospitality boxes. Father Time for the moment sits awkwardly on top of the Mound Stand clock and it is not certain that he will return to his time honoured position on the Grand Stand.

N.B. Some stands, including the Grandstand, were not open for some Middlesex matches in 1998.

Catering and Bars:

On big match days there is plenty of food and drink around much in the style of Royal Ascot and the Chelsea Flow Show .with loads of corporate tentage. In the pavilion after a long wait for eggs and bacon there are beef baps , or chicken, prawn, tuna or cheese sandwiches. Surprisingly the sandwiches have often gone unless you get in early, and no surprise at all that there are always queues in the bars inside and outside members' areas.

For major matches, in the food market at the Nursery End champagne is at £31.50 to go with the lobster and sea food salads. There are good prawn mayonnaise baps at £2.70 or fast food/slow service for chicken, steak and chips, pasties and pies. The most relaxing breakfasts are at the Hilton Hotel or Lord's Tavern otherwise the clever times to eat inside Lord's on big match days are at 9.15 a.m. or around mid afternoon at the Nursery End.

Lord's and The Oval have been the two Test grounds least troubled by hooliganism and believe that closing bars without warning is an important contributory factor. Bringing your own picnic and meeting friends in the Coronation Garden behind the Warner is still best but standing room only these days.

The fast food, sandwiches and snacks are good quality but more expensive than at most other grounds. There is also a new restaurant in the Warner Stand, offering lunches and teas. For Middlesex members there is usually a hot lunch and snacks available in the Middlesex Room.

Shops:

The Lord's shop at the Nursery end of the ground is spacious, well stocked with a wide range of cricket equipment and good quality merchandise, cricketing memorabilia and an extensive selection of hard and paper back cricket books. It is the best shop on the circuit and open all the year round. MCC members have their own rather murky caravan near the Grace Gates for their unique regalia, with a new line in egg and bacon coloured pyjamas being promised for lady members in the near future.

The Middlesex office behind the pavilion sells Middlesex clothing and souvenirs and a few books.

Museum:

The Museum and Library accommodate the greatest collection of archives, records, books, painting and numerous memorabilia about the game. The library is for MCC Members only but all cricket lovers should visit the museum at least once. The Museum is open on match days only until 5.00 p.m., or can be seen as part of the Lords tours. It is in the tennis court block behind pavilion.

General facilities:

Cricket coaching facilities: Indoor school, 0171-432-1014/5. Middlesex have separate indoor school at Finchley.

Cricket nets: Indoor school. Outdoor nets (members only)

Other sporting or recreational facilities on the ground: Tennis court and squash courts (members only) .

Facilities for hire or wider community use at the ground: Contact MCC for details

Ticket office: MCC in club offices at back of pavilion. Middlesex CCC in Middlesex office behind pavilion.

Scoreboards: The old Grandstand scoreboard was a masterpiece of clarity and economy of essential information. It has been replaced by a glowing orange on black board and in a change from the original design moved above the Compton Stand. In 1999 the electronic Mound Stand scoreboard which has not been particularly easy to decipher may have moved on to the roof of the Allen Stand if a planning application is successful. The theory is that best practice dictates that scoreboards should be located on diagonals on Test Match grounds, but unless your seat is somewhere in the middle you will only easily be able to see one scoreboard.

From some parts of the Mound and Edrich stands neither scoreboard is visible. There are small electronic boards in these areas that give the score and batsmen's scores, but are no substitute for a full scoreboard.

Toilets: High standard facilities with specially adapted facilities for wheelchair users. The best public toilets are in the Grandstand with more traditional facilities at the Nursery End and behind the Allen Stand.
Entrances: No restrictions. Some not open for Middlesex matches.

Facilities and access for people with disabilities:
Guide dogs allowed. Price reductions for wheelchair users for Test Matches and for companions. No reductions for Middlesex matches.
Wheelchair access to the ground: Yes
Designated car parking available inside the ground: Yes, but limited.
Viewing areas inside the ground for people using wheelchairs: In Mound stand and Warner stand.
Ramps to provide easy access to bars and refreshment outlets: Yes

Travel:
Road restrictions on match days: All street parking is controlled. Limited free parking on Sundays (not major matches).
Car parking: Extremely limited at ground. Some private car parks nearby, (see below). *Information:* Master Park: 0800-243348.
NCP Marylebone Road Underground Car Park near Baker Street, W1. Tel: 0171-935-6078. Buses 13,82, 113, 139, 189, 274
NCP Kilburn Square Kilburn High Road NW6
Tel: 0171-328-5500. Buses 98, 16 to St John's Wood Road , NW6.
NCP Bilton Towers Great Cumberland Place Marble Arch London, W1 Tel: 0171-723 8840. Buses 82 (to Lord's), 16 (to St John's Wood Road)
NCP Portman Square Garage, Gloucester Place W1. Tel: 0171-935-5310.
Buses 13, 82, 113, 139, 189, 274
NCP Hyde Park Underground Car Park, Park Lane, W1.
Tel:0171-262 -1814. Buses 82 (to Lord's), 16 (to St John's Wood Road)
ML Car Parks Ltd Church Street, Penfold Street NW8.
Tel: 0171-723 -5148. Buses 6, 98 (to St John's Wood) 139, 189 (to Lord's) or 10 minute walk to Ground
MC Parking Ltd Acacia Car Park, Kingsmill Terrace NW8. Tel 0171 722 1404. By St John's Wood Station 5 minutes walk to Ground
MC Parking Ltd Bell Street London, NW1 (by Edgware Road Bakerloo Station). Tel: 0171-723-6777. Buses 6, 98, 16 (to St John's Wood Road)
Parking in central London can be expensive. Contact the car park in advance to check price and availability. Otherwise use public transport!
Our thanks to the MCC for providing information on parking.

Nearest station: St John's Wood (London Underground).
Information: 0171-222-1234.
Buses: 13, 82, 113, 139 and 274. 6, 98 and 16 to St John's Wood Road.
Information: 0171-222-1234
Tourist information: 0839-123456 (premium rate). Tourist information centres at Victoria and Liverpool Street stations, plus Heathrow airport.

Road directions:
Lord's is on the A41, at the junction with St. John's Wood Road (A5205). From central London, take the A501 inner ring road, and turn north at Gloucester Place (A41). This leads directly to Lord's.
From the M1: at end of motorway turn left onto North Circular (A406). Stay in left hand lanes, and follow signs for A41, going onto roundabout, taking right turn onto A41 . Stay on A41 until reaching Lord's.
From A1: Use A1 until A41 forks off to right, stay on A41, and as above.

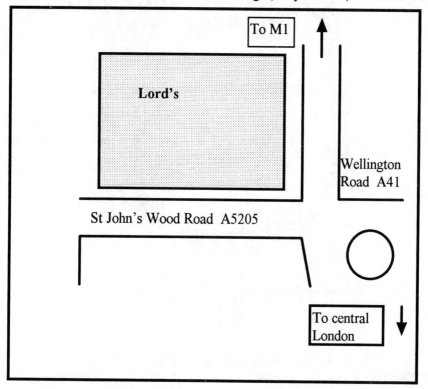

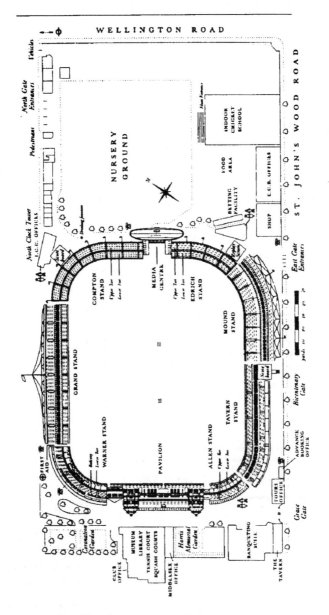

Lord's plan courtesy of the MCC.

N.B. The full name of the new Media Centre is the Nat West Media Centre

Lord's - The Nat West Media Centre (RO)

Feet up at Derby (RO)

Derbyshire CCC
Derby - County Ground

Address: County Ground, Nottingham Road, Derby, DE21 6DA
Capacity: 9,000
Telephone: 01332-383211   **Fax:** 01332-290251
Ticket office: As above
Rapid Cricketline: 0891-567501

Description and Historical Comment:
First used 1863 and in 1868 South Derbyshire defeated the Australian Aborigines who were the first touring side ever to visit England. Once known as the Racecourse Ground the cricket ground occupies part of the former Derby racecourse. The grandstand, copper-domed cupola and stables remain and are eccentric and abandoned in a curious collection of permanent and temporary buildings.

The early days of Derbyshire cricket were inconsistent with some considering them champion county in 1874 as they were unbeaten with only four fixtures when the title went to the side losing the least matches. But results deteriorated and the county lost their first class status in 1887 before regaining it in 1894 and finishing fifth in 1895. 'The Demon' Spofforth was their most famous name who emigrated to England in 1888, married a local girl and played for Derbyshire for three seasons. He also uncovered the dishonesty of Samuel Richardson who defrauded the county of most of their money during the 1890s.

In 1920 they lost 17 out of 18 matches (the other being abandoned without a ball being bowled !!) but by the mid 1930's they were third and then second before all round teamwork famously won the title for them in 1936. Pope and Copson, followed after the war by Jackson and Gladwin were great fast bowlers before Derbyshire went into decline again during the 1970s. But a thrilling Nat West trophy win in 1981 and Benson & Hedges Cup triumph in 1988 were signs of improvement. Players such as Eddie Barlow and more recently Michael Holding and Kim Barnett have played outstanding cricket but produced little in the way of success.

Views from the Boundary:
Members' areas: *Members' pavilion and enclosure.*

The overall spectacle is partly obscured by screens and scaffolding but much improved looking across to the poplars on the Northern side from where people view from their cars or deckchairs and are nearest to the playing area. The Lund Pavilion means that the players no longer have to change in the jockey's changing rooms, there are good viewing areas for members and the Moss Room contains a bar and a players dining room. There are the tiered Streetly and Butterley Stands on the southern side for the general public. The racecourse grandstand is available for members.

Catering and Bars:
The members' bar in the pavilion serves hot and cold food but best place on the ground is Carol's Kabin in front of the trees for whom the queues form well before lunch time. Delicious egg, bacon, sausage baps with mushrooms and burgers mixed how you want them for under £2.

Shops:
A tiny club shop behind the pavilion has clothing and merchandise, the Derbyshire year book and Playfair Annual. There is a Supporters Club shop with a bar and seating area and included a number of second hand romantic fiction and crime paper backs, one or two cricket books and old cricket magazines.

General Facilities:
Cricket coaching facilities: Contact club.
Cricket nets: Yes.
Other sporting or recreational facilities on the ground: Indoor sports hall: 01332-383211.
Facilities for hire or wider community use at the ground: Contact club.
Other sporting recreational / leisure activities: Football and cricket pitches by ground.
Ticket office: Club office.
Scoreboards: One new scoreboard opposite the grandstand; next to the old one which accommodates radio and TV commentators.

Toilets: Good facilities for members in the Lund pavilion; one good public toilet on the ground.

Entrances: The main entrance is from the Pentagon roundabout straight onto the substantial parking area adjoining the ground.

Facilities and access for people with disabilities:
Visually handicapped people pay reduced admission although carers pay full price; no special commentary is available.

Wheelchair access to the ground: Yes

Designated car parking available inside the ground: Beside South stand.

Viewing areas for people using wheelchairs: On grass at northern end.

Ramps to provide easy access to bars and refreshment outlets: Most bars and refreshment areas are accessible.

Travel:
Car parking: Large car park at ground.

Nearest station: Derby.

Buses: R5,R2 to Grandstand stop. Bus station in town centre. Information: 01332-292200

Tourist information: Derby TIC, Assembly Rooms, Market Place, DE1 3AH. 01332-255802. Fax: 01332-256137.

Road directions:
By Pentagon roundabout, on A61(Sir Frank Whittle Road) and A52. Well signposted from Derby ring road.

From M1: J28 follow signs to Derby A38 or A6 to Pentagon roundabout where the ground adjoins Frank Whittle Road and Nottingham Road.

From east: M1 J25 follow signs to Derby A52 and A61 to Pentagon roundabout.

From South; M1 J24 follow signs Derby A6 then A52 ring road to Spondon then A61 to Pentagon roundabout.

From West: A52, A38 and A5111 to ring road then A61 to Pentagon

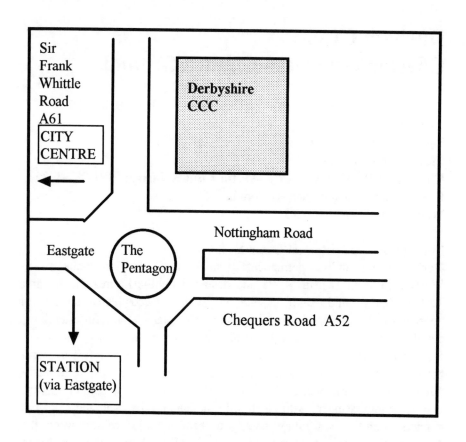

Sir Frank Whittle Road A61

CITY CENTRE

←

Derbyshire CCC

Eastgate

The Pentagon

Nottingham Road

Chequers Road A52

STATION (via Eastgate)

HIGH PEAK CRICKET SOCIETY
Established 1994
Chairman: G.WOOLLEY *Secretary:* R.H.WOOD
Treasurer: J.J.BRAY
Committee: D. Fletcher David Hibbert, Duncan Hibbert, D. Washbrook, F. M. Bullough
Meetings are held at regular intervals during the winter
A Buffet Supper is available at a moderate cost.
For information please contact:- R.H. Wood,
3 Orchard Avenue, Whaley Bridge, High Peak, SK23 7AH
Telephone: 01663 732779

Durham CCC
Chester-le-Street - County Ground

Address: Riverside, Chester-le-Street, County Durham, DH3 3QR
Capacity: 8,000
Telephone: 0191-387-1717   **Fax:** 0191-387-1616
Ticket office: As above
Clubline: 0891-525140   **Austin's Bar & Bistro:** 0191-388-3335
E-mail: marketing@durham-ccc.org.uk
Website: durham-ccc.org.uk

Description and Historical Comment:
Durham's outstanding permanent ground staged its first game against Warwickshire on 18 May 1995 and designed for the future, is a potential Test Match ground. Built in modules with two completed so far, the approach to the Riverside signals positive thinking and careful attention to detail in the planning and development of a cricket ground.

F.S. Ashley Cooper in *Nottingham Cricket and Cricketers* refers to cricket being played in Durham County in 1751 and the present club were formed in 1882. A founder member of the Second Class Counties competition in 1895, they were joint winners with Norfolk in the inaugural season and eight time winners overall. First minor county to beat a major county when they defeated Yorkshire at Harrogate in 1973. First class status presented leadership and playing problems in the early days, but strong support from members and a crop of good young players led by David Boon give hope for more consistency and the target is a place in the Premier Division in 2000.

Views from the Boundary:
Members' areas: *Don Robson Pavilion, County stand, members' enclosure.*

The Riverside is on the edge of town, well sign posted to adjacent car parks. It's positive attitude towards disabled people is immediately visible with designated car parking and attendants available if required.

14

The Don Robson pavilion complex and grandstand provides excellent facilities for members with views towards Lumley Castle on the hills. The design is based on a traditional cricket ground with first floor balcony viewing from the spacious member's lounge and bar area with hospitality suites including the Colin Milburn lounge above. At ground level is the popular Austin's Bar and Bistro, club shop, and health club with lifts serving all floors.

There is bucket seated terracing at the Lumley and Finchale Ends for the general public.

Views are good from all round the ground although the unfinished parts at the scorebox end feel like a bit of a wasteland with temporary buildings and unmade up areas.

Catering and Bars:
Service in the members lounge is brisk queuing in a cafeteria with in house catering providing substantial steak and kidney pies, cannelloni and hot stotty baps all served with loads of chips; no sign of the ham and pease pudding sandwiches of Stockton fame. Dining tables are set at either end with plenty of room around the bar area in what is really a conference or special occasion facility. A few screens, flowers on the tables and photographs around the walls to give the personal rather the collegiate touch would make it even better.

Austin's Bar & Bistro is open all week, with lunch available from 12 midday to 2.30 p.m.

Refreshments around the ground are hardly a find with uninspiring looking coffee booths and a kiosk serving hot dogs, hamburgers and sandwiches

Shops:
The large club shop has cricket equipment and Durham CC merchandise with a few current best selling cricket books and Wisden and Playfair with cricket magazines.

General facilities:
Cricket coaching facilities: Yes. In the winter in association with the Durham Cricket Association.
Cricket nets: Yes. In summer - selected members in conjunction with county squads.

Other sporting or recreational facilities on the ground: No. Next door is Riverside complex with other sporting facilities.

Facilities for hire or wider community use at the ground: Pavilion available all year round for weddings, seminars, product launches etc.

Other sporting recreational / leisure activities: Separately run health club available to members and non members.

Ticket office: Club office.

Scoreboards: There is a very good modern high tech scoreboard, white on black with a clock which, although it is clear to see took time to work out the key aspects of information.

Toilets: Very good modern facilities for members including disabled people in main pavilion and hospitality areas. Toilets for the general public including disabled people behind the scoreboard.

Entrances: No restrictions.

Facilities and access for people with disabilities:

The best in the country with access to all areas for people with disabilities. Viewing points for wheelchairs are all over the ground and disabled people on the ground particularly appreciated staff attitudes. Although some liked the designated spaces others would have preferred spaces for wheelchairs on the terraces so that they could sit with their friends or companions; integration rather than separation is the name of the game. An Induction Loop System is located in the Members Lounge for Members who are hard of hearing. Guide dogs are allowed on the ground. Admission concessions for carers for some matches. Commentary service to be piloted in 1999.

Wheelchair access to the ground: Yes.

Designated car parking available inside the ground: No.

Viewing areas for people using wheelchairs: Yes - designated areas in all parts of the ground.

Ramps to provide easy access to bars and refreshment outlets: Yes.

Travel:

Car parking: Members & General Public: ample parking in vicinity of Ground.

Nearest station: Local trains to Chester-le-Street. Main line to Durham (15 minutes by taxi) or Newcastle (20 minutes by taxi).

Buses: Walk down station Road to Front Street. Northern Bus Company 37, 21a, 180, 231, 778, 775. Information: 0191-386-4411 x 3337
Tourist information: Durham TIC, Market Place, Durham,DH1 3NJ. 0191-384-3720.

Road directions:
From A1(M) junction 63, take A167 (Shields Road) south from roundabout. Stay on A167 at roundabout, which becomes Park Road North, then Park Road Central. Left at roundabout into Ropery Lane, then right, into Riverside complex.

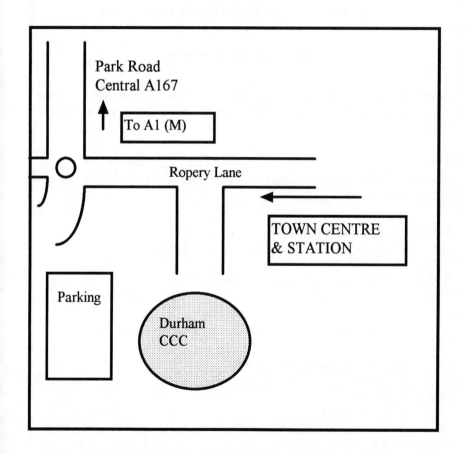

The Durham and North East Branch
of
The Cricket Society

welcomes the publication of this book which provides useful information for those who often travel long distances to watch cricket.

The Durham and North East Branch is the "youngest" of the branches of The Cricket Society. It was formed in 1995 and has an enthusiastic membership.

Meetings are held on:
The first Thursday of each month from October to March.
Venue: the Members' Lounge of Durham County Cricket Club, The Riverside, Chester-le-Street, Co. Durham
Time: 7.30 p.m.

Guests are most welcome - come and join us!

For further information, contact:
Hon. Secretary: Professor Roy Storer
164, Eastern Way
Darras Hall, Ponteland
Newcastle upon Tyne NE20 9RH
Telephone & fax: 01661-823286

18

DURHAM COUNTY CRICKET CLUB

A FIRST CLASS VENUE
Outstanding hospitality facilities at Riverside

An ideal setting for

Corporate Entertaining
Conference and Banqueting facilities for up to 330 people

Easy access from the A1(M) and plenty of car parking

For further information call 0191 387 1717

Durham County Cricket Club, County Ground, Riverside
Chester-le-Street, Co. Durham, DH3 3QR
Official website: www.durham-ccc.org.uk

19

Essex CCC
Chelmsford - County Ground

Address: New Writtle Street, Chelmsford, Essex, CM2 0PG
Capacity: 7,000
Telephone: 01245-252420   **Fax:** 01245-491607
Ticket office: As above   **Rapid Cricketline:** 0930-161203
Ticket information & prospects for play: 01245-287921 (answerphone)
Cricket school: 01245-266794 **Fax:** 01245-491607

Description and Historical Comment :
Although playing mostly at Leyton, Essex were always nomadic, taking their travelling circus around nine grounds from Ilford and Romford to Colchester, Westcliff and Southend on Sea. Every bit of ground equipment including the famous double decker buses that accommodated the scoreboard and the ladies lavatory were moved around the county.

Thanks to a generous interest free loan from Warwickshire Supporters' Club, Essex acquired Chelmsford in 1967 and the ground became county headquarters. It is next door to the former Chelmsford City FC ground.

The River Can passes alongside at the Town end beside Central Park and it is possible to have lunch by the river on the picnic benches.

Essex achieved first class status in 1894, Perrin was the batting star and despite never playing for England Kortright was a very fast bowler who between 1885 and 1888 clean bowled 226 of his 319 victims.

J.W.H.T. Douglas was a top class batsman and swing bowler who captained England and Essex before and after the first World War. He was an outstanding boxer and international footballer and tragically drowned trying to rescue his father when the SS Oberon sank in a collision.

Maurice Nichols and Ken Farnes were dominating fast bowlers before World War II and Trevor "barnacle" Bailey a splendid all rounder after it.

But it took Essex until 1979 and the days of Fletcher and Gooch to lead the way to winning five championships, numerous cups and much else besides; an outstanding team of the last two decades.

Views from the Boundary:
Members areas: *Pavilion, open seating by Pavilion, Tom Pearce stand, stand above River Restaurant.*

Chelmsford is an attractive modernised ground ten minutes from the town centre. It has a very good atmosphere even when there are only a few people on the ground. With a large and enthusiastic membership and local cricket society, this is very much a members club and ground, with limited space, and fewer facilities, for the general public.

The pavilion has the players accommodation on the first floor with a members bar and lounge below. Most stands offer a good view with the Tom Pearce stand and River Restaurant Stand providing open seating and the best view of all. The lower tier of the Tom Pearce stand is no smoking and pillars there slightly restrict views but this is only a problem at big matches.

All other seating is open, tiered and cramped with narrow walkways around the ground and everything is squeezed into a very small site.

Catering and Bars:
The members only River restaurant has a Carvery and snacks, with two course meals. The tea bars offer pies, burgers, chips, tea and coffee. For non members, the tea bar is behind main scoreboard and for members by the pavilion. At lunch time, try the picnic benches by river (near River restaurant). There are bars for members in the pavilion and non members near the main scoreboard.

Shop:
By pavilion (you need a pass out during play). The Essex shop is a marvellous example of what can be achieved with enthusiasm and ingenuity despite adverse conditions in a cramped and poorly ventilated building. Serious choices for informed cricket book lovers, videos, magazines, newspapers, cricket equipment and memorabilia crammed into tight corners. Run by cheerful and responsive staff who deserve better and must hope that a new site is high on the County Development Plan.

Scorecards: Sold from hut behind pavilion.

Museum: None. There is a library behind pavilion, and old photos etc. in pavilion.

General facilities:
Cricket coaching facilities: Yes. Available all year in indoor school.
Cricket nets: Yes
Facilities for hire or wider community use at the ground: Rooms for weddings, exhibitions, conferences etc.
Ticket office: County Office by pavilion
Scoreboards: Main one in corner opposite pavilion. Also small one by shop / executive suite.
Toilets: Behind pavilion, behind scoreboard and others.
Entrances: No restrictions

Facilities and access for people with disabilities:
Disabled members who cannot watch without a carer are entitled to apply for a free membership ticket for their carer. No reduced admission for visually impaired people. Guide dogs allowed - contact club in advance. Some admission charge reductions for carers with members.
Wheelchair access to the ground: Yes.
Designated car parking available inside the ground: Yes.
Viewing areas for people using wheelchairs: Yes - by shop / press box.
Ramps to provide easy access to bars and refreshment outlets: Yes.
Toilets: 1) Behind marquees / public covered seating. 2) Behind pavilion.

Travel:
Car parking: At ground - members only. Public pay car park in New Whittle St - gets full for 1 day or bigger games. Overflow parking at former Chelmsford City Football Club ground - free. Otherwise try the town centre.
Nearest station: Chelmsford.
Buses: Bus station 0.5 miles from ground. Information: 01245-262828. 100 along New London Road, or Eastern National 32.
Tourist information: Chelmsford TIC, E Block, County Hall, Market Rd, CM1 1GG. 01245-283400. Fax: 01245-430705.

Road directions:
Ground is in town centre, near the junction of the A138 with the B1007 (New London Road). Access by car from the B1007, and then turn into New Writtle Street. Next door to former Chelmsford City FC ground.

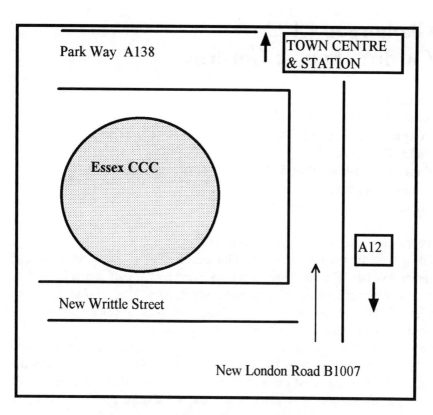

Park Way A138

TOWN CENTRE & STATION

Essex CCC

A12

New Writtle Street

New London Road B1007

Top view at Chelmsford (PDL)

Glamorgan CCC
Cardiff - Sophia Gardens

Capacity: 5,500
Address: Sophia Gardens, Cardiff, CF1 9XR
Telephone: 01222-343478   **Fax:** 01222-377044
Ticket Office: As above
Rapid Cricketline: 0891-567504
E-mail: glam@ecb.co.uk
Website: www.glamorganccc.cricket.org

Description and Historical Comment:

Glamorgan first played at Sophia Gardens in 1967 in the match against the Indian tourists. The club now own the ground by the Taff in a delightful tree surrounded rural setting. The ground takes its name from Sophia, the second wife of the second Marquess of Bute and was a place for people to promenade and listen to the band on summer evenings.

Glamorgan CCC was formed on 6 July 1886 and attained first class status in 1921, with first season performances attracting Wisden's curt observation that their entry into first class cricket was not justified by their results. But with the indefatigable Wooller, Clay and Parkhouse they won their first championship in 1948, and unbeaten in the summer the 'happy team' captained by Tony Lewis and inspired by Majid won again in 1969. In 1997 led by the wonderfully talented but capricious Maynard the enthusiastic supporters were justly rewarded with more daffodil days.

Views from the Boundary:

Members areas: *Pavilion, Vice Presidents stands.*

Sophia Gardens is situated just off Cathedral Road, next to the National Sports Centre for Wales and near the city centre. The pavilion and club offices are at right angles to the pitch with additional small stands for members and vice presidents and larger public stands at the river and Cathedral Road ends.

Entrance to the ground is from either end of Cathedral Road with car parking on the Rugby ground at the top end. Although there are more expensive levels of membership offering different privileges full membership at £25 for 1998 was a real bargain. In addition to the normal reciprocal arrangements when teams are playing each other, Glamorgan, Gloucestershire, Worcestershire and Somerset, offer membership privileges to each other's members, whoever the visitors are.

Best views are from the pavilion and vice presidents stands; more peaceful in the latter areas as well as in the well informed River Stand. The Cathedral End stand has been known to accommodate tediously boring opposition serenaders at one day games who need removing sooner rather than later.

Catering and Bars:
Very good club bar for members on top of pavilion and players' reports say that the dining room is the best on the circuit, although it seems to be aimed at corporate entertainees because you have to wait until they've finished and miss half of the second session. The rest could hardly be described as a choice with nondescript sandwiches, pasties wrapped in cellophane paper and tea and biscuits for both members and the general public. There are hamburgers and chips and other similar food on the ground but bring your own may be best.

Shops:
The space constraints of the Glamorgan souvenir caravan displaying cricket merchandise and a few coffee mugs make it almost impossible for more than two or three at a time to look around and a new shop must be a priority in the development plan. See the club's website for more information.

Museum:
Not open on match days and viewing is by appointment.

General facilities:
Cricket coaching facilities: Yes (not match days).
Cricket nets: Yes (players only).
Other sporting or recreational facilities on the ground: Hockey.
Facilities for hire or wider community use at the ground: No.
Other sporting recreational / leisure activities: Tennis courts and other facilities next door, at Welsh Institute of Sport.
Ticket office: Club office.

Scoreboards: There is a high standard computerised scoreboard which does its best to keep members amused with unintentional errors followed by rueful apologies on the public address.

Toilets: Decent facilities for members in the pavilion and the main general public toilet is near the main entrance and includes facilities for people with disabilities. Otherwise temporary toilets behind the pavilion for big games.

Entrances: Either end of Cathedral Road or behind the pavilion. No restrictions.

Facilities and access for people with disabilities:
No reduced admission for visually impaired people. Guide dogs allowed.
Wheelchair access to the ground: Yes.
Designated car parking available inside the ground: Yes.
Viewing areas for people using wheelchairs: Yes - Rugby Ground end or by pavilion.
Ramps to provide easy access to bars and refreshment outlets: Yes.

Travel:
Car parking: Field next to ground, or at Sports Centre complex.
Nearest station: Cardiff Central, 1 mile from ground
Buses: 62c, 65c from station. Also 25, 56. Information: 01222-396521. Also other buses to Cathedral Road.
Tourist information: Cardiff Central Station, Central Square, Cardiff CF1 1QY. 01222-227281.

Road directions:
On Cathedral Road (A4119), just north of junction with A4161. From M4, junction 29, A48 towards city centre. Turn off A48 towards city centre onto A4119, left to Cathedral Road (still A4119). Then Sophia Gardens is on left. From city centre take A4161, turn right onto Cathedral Road (A4119) and Sophia Grounds is on right.

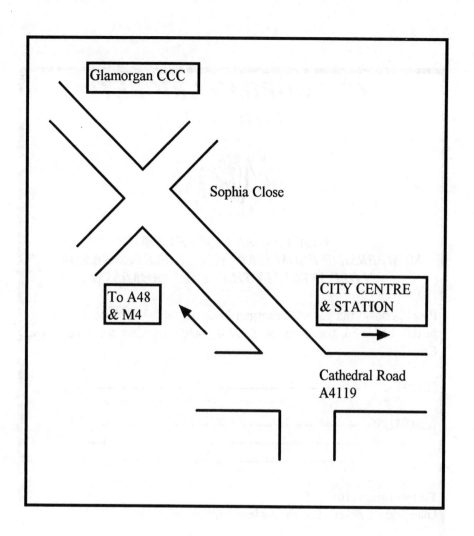

Glamorgan CCC

Sophia Close

To A48
& M4

CITY CENTRE
& STATION

Cathedral Road
A4119

GLAMORGAN CRICKET
MEMBERSHIP

GLAMORGAN CRICKET 1999
MEMBERSHIP FROM £30.00 PER ADULT PER SEASON ~
AN OPPORTUNITY THAT CAN'T BE MISSED!

Please enlist me as a Glamorgan 'member' and I enclose a cheque / postal order in the sum of £30.00, made payable to: Glamorgan Cricket

NAME : ---

ADDRESS: ---

Please return to:
Glamorgan Cricket, Sophia Gardens, Cardiff CF1 9XR

FOR DETAILS OF OTHER CATEGORIES
OF MEMBERSHIP, PLEASE CALL:
(01222) 343478 OR (01222) 409380

Photocopy this form if you do not want to cut the book

The pavilion at Abergavenny (RO)

The bat workshop at Leicester (PDL)

Gloucestershire CCC
Bristol - Sun Alliance County Ground

Address: Sun Alliance County Ground, Nevil Road, Bristol, BS7 9EJ
Capacity: 4,500
Telephone: 0117-910-8000   **Fax:** 0117-924-1193
Ticket office: As above   **Club shop:** 0117-942-8180
Rapid Cricketline: 0891-567505
Catering Manager:0117-910-8000
Gold Bond Cashline: 0117-910-8020

Description and Historical Comment:
The Ashley Down Ground was first used by Gloucestershire against
Warwickshire on 23 May 1889. Although the home side were not to achieve
first class status until 1895, they won by 68 runs. The ground was sold to the
Fry's chocolate company in 1916. Various additions have been made to the
original 1880s pavilion. The main entrance is through the Grace Gates from
Nevil Road. or through a side gate from the Bristol College car park. Recent
ground improvements include an indoor school, a new scorers' and press
box, and an enlarged and modern shop. The replacement of the Jessop Stand
is planned for opening in time for the World Cup in May 1999.
The great names and memories of Grace, Jessop, Hammond and
subsequently Charlie Parker, Goddard, Graveney, Zaheer, Proctor and
Walsh have illuminated a somewhat pedestrian cricket ground. The
Champion Grace, scorer of 54,896 runs and 126 hundreds, 2,876 wickets
and 877 catches changed the nature of the game. He was the first to
recognise the equal importance of forward and back play and achieved his
success on generally poor pitches. Jessop, "The Croucher", low over the bat,
was the hitter at pace and Hammond, between the wars the supreme
plunderer of 50,551 runs and 167 centuries.
Gloucestershire historically never quite had the fast bowlers to clinch the
title, although finishing second in 1939 and again in 1947, when there was a
close battle with Middlesex. But with Alleyne's all round talents, Russell,
Smith and signs of consistency among some of the young players the gossip
in the Hammond Room encourages good omens for the future

Views from the Boundary:
Members areas: *Pavilion, Members' enclosure.*

There is now an air of change within the Ashley Down ground, spaciously established in the Bristol suburbs away from the noise and tower blocks in the city centre. The Muller orphanage buildings (now part of City of Bristol College) and neat Victorian terrace houses surround three sides. The ground is not easily found through narrow car parked side streets.

The pavilion, much altered from the original, is set back from the edge of the ground and is a place that you can easily get lost in, although the staff don't seems to mind. The best view for members is besides the pavilion, although the new Jessop Stand will include high level seating as well as a Media centre and possibly the relocated Museum.

Bucket seats under cover or in open terracing are around the ground and 'bring your own' provides good viewing on the tennis courts side or behind the bowler's arm at the Ashley Down end. Stewards at Bristol tend to look worried and complain about lack of support for either home or away teams; the exception is the jovial and raucous Bristol Evening Post vendor selling the late edition.

Catering and Bars:
The Grace Room is the main function room and was up graded and re-decorated for the 1998 season. Hammond Room food for members is predictable with sausage, beans and chips and sometimes disappointing with baps containing more bread than bacon and indeterminate shepherd's or vegetarian pies which could pass for either.

Good presentation with eye catching labelling could be improved, as at most grounds. A routine selection of sandwiches are hidden at the back of the fridge which is a bit off putting, but a short lived improvement was to serve tea and coffee in china mugs; there were probably too many breakages!!

For the general public there is the beefburger and chips formula and not much else. The end of the old Jessop Tavern will be mourned by the long suffering loyalists and a few college students who enjoyed the Supporters Club atmosphere. Let's hope the new stand does not become an up market emporium for corporate hospitality and that small boys will still be allowed to bowl to their fathers in front of it during the intervals

Shop:
The spacious new shop concentrates on cricket equipment and merchandise but, besides a decent selection of new books, incorporates Mr Faulkner's very good section of second hand cricket books.

Museum:
The well displayed museum, currently in the pavilion, contains displays of memorabilia, photographs and many other items of Gloucestershire cricket interest and history. Open during matches.

General facilities:
Cricket coaching facilities: Yes.
Cricket nets: Yes - all year.
Other sporting or recreational facilities on the ground: Squash, gym, tennis.
Facilities for hire or wider community use at the ground: Yes - contact club.
Ticket office: Club office.
Scoreboards: Two electronic scoreboards both operated from the main box should make things easy but apparently recognising the players and decoding the more obscure umpiring signals is the problem.
Toilets: Good modern ones in the pavilion and two on either side of the ground all providing facilities for disabled people. Those on the college side have improved with upgrading and repainting and the same is required of the dingy outhouse opposite the shop. Better still, replace and modernise to include ladies and disabled facilities to replace the temporary building next to the tennis courts.

Facilities and access for people with disabilities:
Reduced admission for visually impaired people for some matches. Guide dogs allowed. Phone club for further information.
Wheelchair access to the ground: Yes.
Designated car parking available inside the ground: Yes.
Viewing areas for people using wheelchairs: Yes.
Ramps to provide easy access to bars and refreshment outlets: Yes.
Toilets: In pavilion and both sides of ground.

Travel:
Car parking: Inside ground and in playing field beside ground.
Nearest station: Bristol Parkway or Bristol Temple Meads (main line), Montpelier (local trains)
Buses: From Bristol Fashion (by bus station): 71,72,73,74,75,76 and 77. From Bristol Parkway: 73. From Bristol Temple Meads: 8 & 9 to bus station, then as above. Information: 0117-955-5111
Tourist information: Bristol TIC, St Nicholas Church, St Nicholas St, BS1 1UE. Tel: 0117-926-0767. Fax: 0117- 929-7703.

Road directions:
M32 take junction 2, for Fishponds and Horfield. Take Muller Road exit (3rd if coming from M4). Turn left into Ralph Rd (turning opposite bus station). Turn left at end of road onto Ashley Down Rd, then almost immediately right into Kennington Avenue. Turn left at end of road to ground.
If coming from A38, turn into Nevil Road which leads to Kennington Avenue and the ground

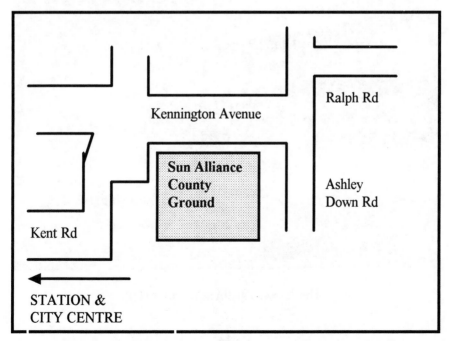

The Jessop Tavern at Bristol (RO)

Hampshire CCC
Southampton - County Ground

Address: Northlands Road, Southampton, Hants, SO15 2UE
Capacity: 5,000
Telephone: 01703-333788   **Fax:** 01703-330121
Ticket office: As above.
Hampshire Cricket Line: 0336-500141. **Faxback:** 0336-421723
County Club (includes restaurant, gym & squash): 01703-334393
Website: www.hampshire.cricket.org
E.Mail: hants@ecb.co.uk

Description and Historical Comment:
Although cricket really began in Kent and Sussex legend has it that it all started in the mid 18th century in Hambledon immediately prior to the founding of the MCC in 1787. The County Cricket Club was not formed until 1863 and achieved first class status in 1895 winning their first championship match against Somerset by 11 runs.

The first county match on the ground was against Derbyshire in 1885 and the present pavilion was built in 1895 with more buildings in the first part of the twentieth century. In 1896/7 Southampton FC played there before moving to their present ground. Before the first war Philip Mead scorer of 48,892 runs and 153 centuries and together with Alec Kennedy, George Brown and Jack Newman were the main strength of side. The mulit-talented C.B.Fry; the South African Llewellyn, who bowled the first chinaman, and Lionel Tennyson, helped Hampshire to make steady improvement and famous victories including their great win at Edgbaston in 1922 after being dismissed for 15 runs in the first innings.

But not until 1961 under Colin Ingleby McKensie with the Barbadian Roy Marshall, John Arlott's favourite Henry Horton, Gray, Salisbury and the inimitable Derek Shackleton did they win a championship. They won it again under Richard Gilliat in 1973 and subsequently a Benson and Hedges Cup with Greenidge and Malcolm Marshall in 1988.

Views from the boundary:
Members areas: *Pavilion, part of Northlands Road end.*

The County Ground is in a pleasant suburban setting outside the city centre. It is more a place of history and reminiscence with an ancient pavilion and otherwise plain buildings mainly surrounded by houses and flats with exposed public seating areas. Developments have included the indoor cricket school, County Club (squash and gym) in 1982 and Philip Mead Stand in 1987.The ground includes practice pitches, tennis courts and bowls. The club are now moving to a new venue with a playing field the size of Lords on the edge of the city which will come into use in 2001, so make time for at least one visit to the ground over the next two years.
There are generally good views from public seating areas, but very little under cover. The pavilion has partly restricted views due to roof pillars. The Philip Mead stand is under cover, but has a small capacity.

Catering and Bars:
The County Club has a decent bar, good value meals and hot snacks and is a pleasant place for lunch with the usual selection of sandwiches. In the pavilion, members can choose between fresh ham and cheese salads, fast food and sandwiches and the café by Northlands Road has much of the same.

Shop:
By Philip Mead stand, it has clothing, some books and Hampshire souvenirs etc. It needs a permanent venue to develop further - hopefully this will be included at the new ground. Orders can be placed through the club's website.

General facilities:
Cricket coaching facilities: Yes
Cricket nets: Yes - professionals only in summer. Clubs in winter.
Other sporting or recreational facilities on the ground: Squash, gym, indoor nets (October - April)
Facilities for hire or wider community use at the ground: Restaurant and some conference facilities.
Ticket office: At county office
Scoreboards: Main scoreboard at City end. Also small one.
Toilets: By County Club, scoreboard and by nets.

Facilities and access for people with disabilities:
No reduced admission for visually impaired people. Guide dogs allowed.
Wheelchair access to the ground: Yes.
Designated car parking available inside the ground: Yes.
Viewing areas for people using wheelchairs: Yes. Designated areas.
Ramps to provide easy access to bars and refreshment outlets: No
Toilets: By County Club.

Travel:
Car parking: Ticket holders only at ground. Limited street parking.
Nearest station: Southampton Central
Buses: 5. Information: 01703-224854
Tourist information: Southampton TIC, 9, Civic Centre Rd, S014 7LP.
01703-221106. Fax: 01703-832082.

The Hampshire Cricket Society

SOCIETY SPONSORS

BROOKING KNOWLES & LAWRENCE
BKL   BKL

- 8 Meetings a year with well known speakers
- Annual Buffet Supper
- Regular Newsletter

For more information (including subscriptions) contact the Secretary:

Jack Moore, 85, Kingsway, Chandlers Ford, Eastleigh, Hants S053 1FD.
Tel: 01703-252400

Road directions:
From north take A33 (The Avenue) towards Southampton city centre. Approx. 1.5 miles north of city centre. Turn right into Northlands Road. Ground is signposted. Northlands Road is first turning on right at end of Southampton Common on right-hand side. AA yellow signs from M3/A33 to Northlands Road.

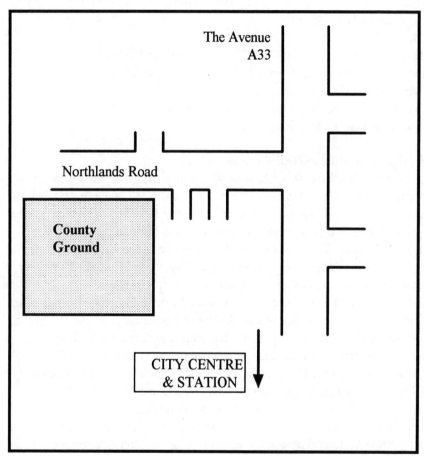

Kent CCC
Canterbury - St. Lawrence Ground

Address: St Lawrence Ground, Old Dover Road, Canterbury, CT1 3NZ
Capacity: 8,000 - including temporary seating for big matches
Telephone: 01227-456886   **Fax:** 01227-762168
Ticket office: As above
Information hotline: 0336-500121.   **Faxback:** 0336-421777
Ames-Levett Sports Centre: 01227-784996. **Fax:** 01227-453130
E.Mail: kent-cricket@msn.com.
E.Mail for Marketing: marketing.kent@ecb.co.uk
Web: www.kentcountycricket.co.uk

Description and Historical Comment:
Kent cricket is where it all began, with the county playing twenty seven matches against Hambledon between 1768 and 1787, winning twelve and losing thirteen with one tie and a draw. From 1834 to 1850 they reigned supreme "with five such mighty cricketers 'twas but natural to win as Felix, Wenman, Hillyer, Fuller Pilch and Alfred Mynn". The Canterbury Festival originated from these times and in a remarkable combination of cricketing, social, theatrical interests and personalities continues today.

Festival week in the sunshine, with marquees around the ground is one of the glorious experiences of the season. A lime tree is uniquely within the playing area, now sadly in terminal decline, but with a replacement sapling ready to maintain the tradition. It is said to have been cleared by a certain Colonel A. C. Watson of Sussex, followed by Constantine and Hooper. But Ladies Day on Thursday continues with elegant hats and the tents alive with the Band of Brothers and Old Stagers as well as the local grandees.

After the Pilch and Mynn era, it was not until 1870 that the arrival of Lord Harris brought remarkable influence, organisation and development to the game in the county and elsewhere. Championship victories in 1906, 1909, 1910 and 1913 proved them to be the best in the country and in addition to the captain, Yardley, the big hitter Thornton, Frank Woolley, JR Mason a brilliant all-rounder, Fielder, together with Ken Hutchings, a superb batsman and the immortal, slow left armer 'Charlie' Blythe with many others, marked a very special Golden Age.

Between the wars Hubble and Ames established the tradition of great Kent wicket keepers followed by Evans and Knott; dynamic A.P.H. Chapman who epitomised attacking cricket and Brian Valentine were outstanding captains: the incomparable Tich Freeman; Marriott and Doug Wright were laughably unorthodox and outstanding leg break bowlers.

But Kent were relatively unsuccessful until after Colin Cowdrey's arrival in the late 1950s revived fortunes with Gillette Cup wins in 1967 and 1974, other frequent one day successes and championships in 1970 and 1977 (joint) and 1978. In the modern era, Kent have more often promised and disappointed remaining in transition rather than producing a winning team.

Views from the Boundary:
Members areas: *Frank Woolley stand, Annexe stand, Pavilion and Colin Cowdrey stand.*

There is much to enjoy at Canterbury, which should include a visit to the cathedral during the day. The pavilion, dating from 1900, renamed the Leslie Chiesman pavilion after internal refurbishment in 1970 is linked to 'the annexe', and with the Leslie Ames enclosure, Frank Woolley Stand and the first floor of the New Stand is available to members only.

The Colin Cowdrey Stand (1986) contains the shop and a public bar on the ground floor as well as the member's area with a grand Executive Suite and the best view in the ground above. The two tiered Concrete Stand (1927) now felicitously renamed the Frank Woolley Stand is the largest covered stand. The pavilion contains memorable paintings, including Chevallier-Taylor's Kent and Lancashire of 1906, and photographs recount the great traditions and personalities of Kent cricket. There is plastic tip up seating around the ground and spectators can bring their own as well. The Colin Blythe memorial is close to the Old Dover Road entrance.

The 1998 scoreboard is technologically sophisticated but almost invisible in bright sunshine and needs white on black or another form of contrast; Major Meakin who donated the old one in 1927 must turn in his grave.

The members areas offer some cover, and the match can be viewed from behind glass in the Colin Cowdrey stand. There is no cover for the public seats, but most offer unrestricted views.

Catering and Bars
Hot meals in The Carvery (in the Colin Cowdrey stand) are good value. As an alternative, with more choice, try The 70s room. The Cornwallis Room in the Colin Cowdrey stand for members also does meals at lunch time and snacks etc. during the day. Lunch menus have plenty of fast food and standard ham, cheese, tuna and egg mayonnaise sandwiches. There are kiosks around the ground serving snacks, tea, coffee and soft drinks. The Lucky Bar in the sports centre does light refreshments.

Shops
Club shop: A new shop at the back of Colin Cowdrey stand, which concentrates on shirts, tee-shirts, some books and videos, Kent souvenirs, including coffee mugs and key rings, as well as sweets and chocolate.
Cricket shop (in sports centre): A good selection of cricket equipment..
Newspaper and scorecard kiosk by sports centre.
Books: During Festival week and some other matches there is a second hand bookseller has a variety of cricket books.

Museum
None. Old photos in Cornwallis Room (Colin Cowdrey stand) and in pavilion.

General facilities
Cricket coaching facilities: Yes - contact club for details.
Cricket nets: Yes.
Other sporting or recreational facilities on the ground: Yes - sports centre 01227-784996.
Facilities for hire or wider community use at the ground: Yes.
Ticket office: Club office.
Scoreboards: One by Annexe stand, other over Leslie Ames stand.
Toilets: Back of Frank Woolley stand, back of pavilion, in Colin Cowdrey stand (members only)and in other stands and parts of ground.
Women: Back of Frank Woolley stand, back of Annexe stand, by Nackington Rd entrance.
Entrances: No restrictions.

Facilities and access for people with disabilities
Some free entry for visually impaired people and companion. Guide dogs allowed. Give club advance warning as soon as possible. Commentary service provided.
Wheelchair access to the ground: Yes.
Designated car parking available inside the ground: Yes. Orange badge holders.
Viewing areas for people using wheelchairs: Yes. Designated area in Frank Woolley stand.
Ramps to provide easy access to bars and refreshment outlets: Yes.
Toilets: Back of Frank Woolley stand, back of Annexe stand, and in indoor cricket school.

Travel
Car parking: Large car park at ground. Limited street parking, restricted 8 a.m. to 4 p.m. weekdays. Also Sunday restrictions. Alternative parking for important matches at Simon Langton Girls Grammar School, off Old Dover Road.
Nearest station: Canterbury East.
Buses: 17. Information: 01227-472082.
Kent Council transport information: 0345-696996
Special transport arrangements on match days: 17 bus from Folkestone.
Tourist information: Canterbury TIC, 34, St Margaret's St, CT1 2TG. 01227-766567. Fax: 01227-459840

Road directions
The ground is well sign posted from the city centre.
From M2: take A2. Pass first Canterbury turn off. Take turn off for Bridge. Turn right, then fork right and follow signs for Canterbury (A290). Turn left into Old Dover Road - ground on left.
From City Centre, take Old Dover Road turn off at roundabout by bus station, and this leads to the ground.
From north, A290, A291 and A28 to city centre, then as above.

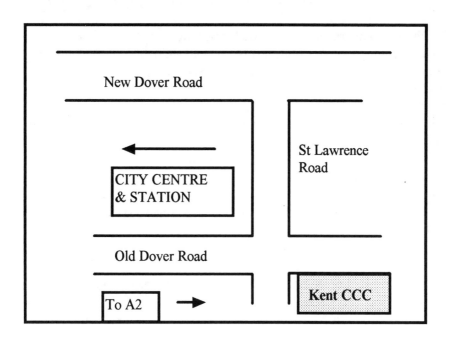

Kent County Cricket Club
St. Lawrence Cricket Ground

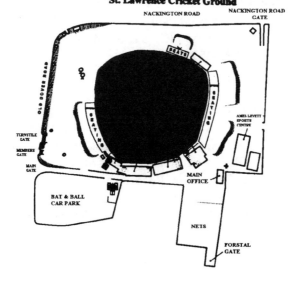

A PERFECT SETTING A PERFECT DAY

KENT COUNTY CRICKET CLUB

1ST CLASS HOSPITALITY

Our hospitality packages are a lavish way to entertain in a unique and picturesque environment.

We offer luxurious marquee and box facilities throughout the season as well as other unique hospitality packages.

KEY DATES IN OUR 1999 CALENDAR

Kent v England Friday 7th May:
Marquee package price £99.00 + VAT per person.

Kent v New Zealand 15th-18th July:
Marquee package price from £85.00 + VAT per person.

KCCC Festival Weeks Tunbridge Wells, Maidstone & Canterbury: Marquee package price £75.00 + VAT per person.

ADVERTISING OPPORTUNITIES

If you need to let people know **"you're out there somewhere"** then let us create media exposure and awareness for your business. The Club has several advertising opportunities to suit all marketing budgets, ranging from perimeter advertising from £1000 to adverts in our annual handbook from £175.00.

For a full marketing pack please contact **ADELE** or **ALISTAIR** in the KCCC Marketing Department:

Telephone: 01227 456886 Fax 01227 762168
Email marketing.kent@ecb.co.uk or
see our information on www.kentcountycricket.co.uk

Lancashire CCC
Old Trafford

Address: Old Trafford, Warwick Road, Manchester, M16 0PX.
Capacity: 21,000
Telephone: 0161-282-4000   **Fax:** 0161-282-4100
Ticket & Membership Office: 0161-282-4040. **Fax:** 0161-873-8353
Club Shop: 0161-282-4050   **Fax:** 0161-282-4100
Lancashire Clubcall: 0891-222244
Conference & Banqueting Centre: 0161-282-4020. **Fax:** 0161-282-4030
Sales & Marketing Department: 0161-282-4061
Cricket Development Office: 0161-282-4016/17
Cricket Centre: 0161-282-4039
Hotel: 0161-874-3333   **Fax:** 0161-874-3399
Website: www.iccc-co.uk

Description and Historical Comment:
Old Trafford has been the principal ground of Lancashire cricket since 1857 and has staged Test Matches since 1884 when England played Australia. The red brick pavilion was built in 1894, used as a medical centre in World War I and bombed during the Second War. Old Trafford is one of the great Test Match grounds, substantially modernised but in character with existing buildings and well known landmarks. The 1981 plan for an hotel on the ground was dropped but one is now being opened for the 1999 season.
The County Cricket Club was formed in 1864, with the first match against Middlesex in 1865 and soon became established as one of the leading championship sides. From the run stealers Barlow and Hornby, great names dominated the early days with Johnny Briggs; Archie Maclaren, scorer of 424 against Somerset in 1895; J.T. Tyldersley; Macdonald and Gregory, the great Australian fast bowlers, and briefly Sydney Barnes who preferred to play league cricket. These were the Cardus heroes who took Lancashire to eight championships and three joint championships between 1881 and 1934, including three times winners between 1926 and 1928. But apart from a joint championship with Middlesex in 1950, the title has since eluded them despite players of the calibre of Washbrook and Statham, Clive Lloyd and

Farouk Engineer and numerous one day Cup and League triumphs through the seventies and eighties.

Views from the Boundary:
Members areas: *Pavilion and members enclosure.*

Old Trafford is an historic ground full of memories and traditions that inspire a tense and exciting atmosphere on important cricketing occasions. This is the ground where, in 1902, Trumper scored a century before lunch; where in 1956, Laker took his 19 wickets against Australia, and in 1961, where Benaud turned the match when England were all set for victory. It is alone among the Test Match grounds in England where the pavilion viewpoint is across the pitch, permitting full sightscreens at both ends.
The Stretford and Warwick Road Ends are among the best known Ends in the game and talk of pigeons and railway stations are part of the folklore of Test Match Special. There was much ground development in the 1980s with The Executive Suite at the Stretford End, and the Neville Cardus Gallery press facilities.
In 1998 for the Test Match against South Africa the ground was half full and lack of interest, bad weather, the football World Cup and alcohol and fancy dress restrictions were all said to be responsible. Apparently more appealing was the first floodlit game with fireworks and a rodeo bull which must be good news if it creates interest in cricket but Maclaren would have turned in his grave!!
The ground is outside the centre of Manchester, but well served by public transport. Look out for stands named after past Lancashire heroes and visit the excellent museum.
Most stands offer unrestricted views. The only public covered area is F stand (lower). G stand is alcohol free. A more panoramic view from the upper tier of F stand.

Catering and bars:
A varied choice for different budgets and culinary tastes with the members' suite in the pavilion offering a bar, hot and cold lunches, pie and chips, sandwiches, light snacks and refreshments. The Tyldesley Suite, by the pavilion and the County restaurant has a similar selection with bookings required on big match occasions (0161-282-4020). The Jubilee Suite has a

bar, cold snacks and light refreshments and there is a fast food bar by A Stand. On Test Match days there are numerous fast food services all around the ground.

Shop:
One of the best county ground shops, situated by A stand. It offers a good selection of shirts, clothing, cricket equipment, souvenirs, books and videos. Also has sweets and drinks.

Museum:
By B Stand. No admission charge. Photos, trophies, souvenirs covering Lancashire and Old Trafford Test Matches. Nineteenth century photos and scorecards. Display on Laker's Test Match versus Australia in 1956. Well worth a visit.

General facilities:
Cricket coaching facilities: For schools and clubs. (Not on match days)
Cricket nets: Indoor cricket school.
Other sporting or recreational facilities on the ground: Squash
Facilities for hire or wider community use at the ground: Conference, exhibition and banqueting facilities, for up to 450 people.
Ticket office: Yes.
Scoreboards: Two - both clear.
Toilets: Most areas of the ground
Entrances: No restrictions
Old Trafford Lodge (68 rooms) opening in April 1999.

Facilities and access for people with disabilities:
Free entry for visually impaired people and companion - depends on match. Check in advance. No guide dogs allowed.
Wheelchair access to the ground: Yes
Designated car parking available inside the ground: Yes for members with reserved car park passes or LCCC disabled parking passes.
Viewing areas for people using wheelchairs: Yes. Designated areas by F stand and A Stand.
Ramps to provide easy access to bars and refreshment outlets: Yes
Toilets: By A and F stand

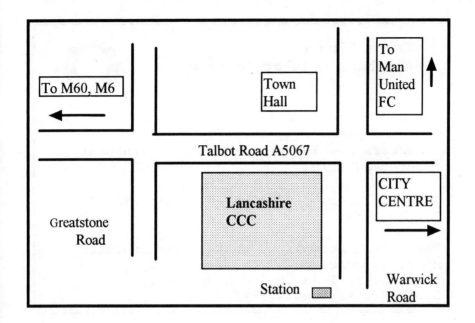

Travel:
Car parking: Plenty at ground. Limited street parking. Additional parking at Kings Road School, Stretford Sports Centre and Manchester United FC for major matches. Town Hall on Sundays.
Nearest station: Old Trafford (Metrolink) Enquiries: 0161-205-2000.
Buses: 0161-228-7811. 115, 52 and 53 near ground, or any bus down Chester Road.
Tourist information: Manchester Visitor Centre, Town Hall Extension, Lloyd St, M60 2LA. 0161-234-3157/3158. Fax: 0161-236-9900.

Road directions:
From M60, take A56 towards Manchester. Fork right onto A5067, Talbot Road, and ground is on right. From city centre, take A56 south, and turn left at junction with Warwick Road. N.B. Ground is 0.25 miles from Manchester United ground - heavy traffic congestion at home matches.

Lancashire & Cheshire Cricket Society

FOUNDED 1953

Monthly meetings at Old Trafford from September to March Members newsletters and information sent out regularly

Subscriptions: Senior £6.00   Junior £3.00
Initial membership fee of £4.00 for new members

For more information, contact The Secretary:
Mr H. W. Pardoe,
"Crantock", 117a Barlow Moor Road,
Didsbury, Manchester M20

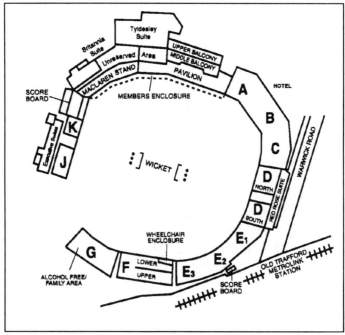

Old Trafford plan courtesy Lancashire CCC

The lime tree at Canterbury (RO)

The pavilion at Old Trafford (PDL)

Leicestershire CCC
Leicester - County Ground

Address: County Ground, Grace Road, Leicester, LE2 8AD
Capacity: 6,500
Telephone: 0116-283-2128   **Fax:** 0116-244-0363
Ticket office: As above.
Conference & Banqueting: 0116-283-7983
Corporate hospitality: 0116-283-1880
Rapid Cricketline: 0891-567509

Description and Historical Comment:
The Grace Road ground opened in 1878, was used by the County from 1884
to 1900 and not again until after World War II. However, it is currently the
only ground used by the county. Leicestershire became first class in 1895 but
led by C.E. De Trafford achieved modest results mainly through the bowlers
Woodcock and particularly Pougher who topped the bowling averages in
1895. D. J. Knight who wrote *The Complete Cricketer* (1906), was an
outstanding batsman who studied Latin and Greek during the intervals and as
a devout lay preacher, prayed for guidance before each innings.
Ewart Astill was the first professional to be appointed the regular captain for
any county in 1935 and together with George Geary, played for England and
dominated Leicestershire cricket between the wars. But it was not until 1950
when Charles Palmer became captain, that things began the change towards
a successful championship and cup winning team with the recruitment of
Willie Watson, Tony Lock and subsequently Ray Illingworth and David
Gower to the side.
Illingworth and then Gower took the County to three Benson and Hedges
Cups and ultimately the Championship in 1975 before progressively good
teamwork in the mid 1990's led to two titles in the last three years.
Although the West Indian Phil Simmons is a star performer, Leicestershire's
main asset has always been self belief as a team with less well known players
making decisive contributions at the right time.

Views from the Boundary:
Members areas: *Pavilion.*

A white fence runs round the boundary and the northern end includes the pavilion, the Fernie and Quorn Suites with tiered seating above for members as well as in the Geary Stand on the Milligan Road side. The Meet is on the Park Hill Drive side providing refreshments for members on the first floor and on the ground floor for the general public. The rest of the ground has tiered seating, the south east corner is covered and there are good views all round the ground. The main scoreboard is next to the Geary Stand and in 1987 a memorial clock tower was added to the building. The bench seats and small stands mix with the new development by the cricket school.

Public areas give unrestricted views. Covered seating on Milligan Road side by scoreboard. Bench seats also offer a good view. If it's cold watch from the bar in The Meet upstairs.

Catering and bars:
The Bennet End Bar, situated in the cricket school, offers drinks, tea and coffee, sandwiches. The Meet offers a good choice of refreshments and bar, hot meals, sandwiches, jacket potatoes, tea and coffee. Food available for members in the pavilion.

Shops:
The M & H Cricket Shop is situated in the cricket school, selling cricket equipment. It includes a bat workshop, the only one we found at a county ground, and worth a visit. The County/souvenir shop is in The Meet and has clothing, souvenirs, hats, ties etc. new and second hand books and sweets.

General facilities:
Cricket coaching facilities: Yes.
Cricket nets: Yes - all year round.
Other sporting or recreational facilities on the ground: No.
Facilities for hire or wider community use at the ground: Yes. Rooms for functions, conferences, meetings etc.
Ticket office: Club office.
Scoreboards: Two. Both give good clear information.
Toilets: Modern ones in cricket school and others around the ground.

Facilities and access for people with disabilities:

Guide dogs allowed. Some price reductions for visually impaired people and people in wheelchairs - notice required. Depends on fixture.

Wheelchair access to the ground: Yes.

Designated car parking available inside the ground: Yes.

Viewing areas for people using wheelchairs: Yes. No specific area, but plenty of flat areas with good views.

Ramps to provide easy access to bars and refreshment outlets: For some, others have small steps, and stewards will assist.

Toilets: In cricket school

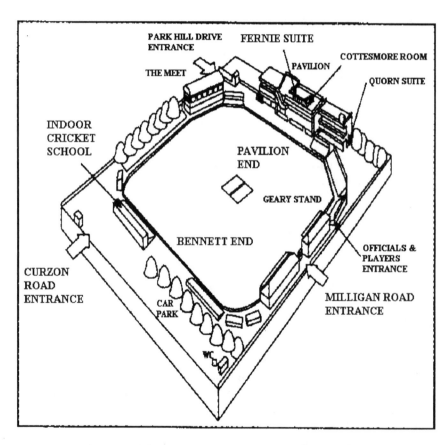

Grace Road plan courtesy of Leicestershire CCC

Travel:
Road restrictions on match days: No parking immediately around ground.
Car parking: Car park at ground, and some street parking.
Nearest station: Leicester.
Buses: 68. Information: 0116-251-1411
Tourist information: Leicester TIC, 7/9 Every Street, Town Hall Sq., LE1 6AG. 0116-265-0555

Road directions:
From M1 junction 21, take A563 towards city centre. Turn left onto A426 (Luterworth Rd), which becomes Aylestone Rd. After 1 mile, turn right into Grace Road. Ground is south of city centre. From city centre, take A426 from inner ring road, turn left into Grace Road. Not always easy to find. Members entrance at Grace Road end. Hawkesbury Road entrance leads to car park and then playing area.

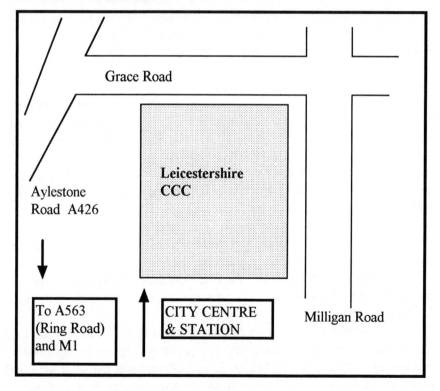

Northamptonshire CCC
Northampton - County Ground

Address: County Cricket Ground, Wantage Road, Northampton, NN1 4TJ
Capacity: 4,500
Telephone: 01604-514455   Fax: 01604-514488
Marketing: 01604-514469
Rapid Cricketline: 0930-161211
Restaurant bookings for match days: Trio Caterers 01604-630376

Description and Historical Comment:
Northampton moved to the County Ground in 1886 and shared it with
Northampton Town FC until 1994, which restricted cricket at the beginning
and end of the season. Joint use undoubtedly contributed to operational
problems for both clubs and a constant struggle for funding for long overdue
improvement and development. The cricket club built a new stand for
members in 1968, and a new pavilion to replace the old Ladies Pavilion in
1979 and now has sole ownership and use of the ground.
Northamptonshire achieved first class status in 1905, were dismissed by
Gloucestershire for the lowest ever first class total of 12 runs in 1907 and
were remarkably runners up to Yorkshire in 1912. The county used only
twelve players, with modest batting but outstanding bowlers including S.G.
Smith, a white West Indian, bowling slow left arm who took 84 wickets at
just over 12 apiece. Between the wars they never held a single figure position
in the championship and were ten times bottom and six times bottom but one;
a dismal record.
Freddie Brown was a strong captain and good all-rounder and improved
things in the early 1950s and at 38 years of age, twelve years since he had
played his last Test captained England against New Zealand. In 1954 Frank
Tyson and Keith Andrew became the first Northants professionals chosen for
an MCC tour of Australia and Tyson spearheaded the attack with Brian
Statham which was to bring back the Ashes.
Northamptonshire's first ever success came when they won the Gillette Cup
in 1976 and were runners up in the championship. They were captained by
Mustaq Mohammed and including Sarfraz Nawaz and the great slow left
arm Indian Captain Bishen Bedi in what was probably their best ever team.

Overseas players have included Jack Walsh and George Tribe, the Australian left arm chinaman and googly bowlers, Alan Lamb, Kapil Dev and Dennis Lillee , all of whom have made impressive contributions to teams that have included Colin Milburn, Wayne Larkins, David Steele and Peter Willey. But limited one day successes with two Nat West trophies and one B & H Cup in the 1980s is all they have had to show for it, and still no championship.

Views from the Boundary:
Members areas: *Pavilion. Top tier life members & vice presidents only.*

The ground now feels like a cricket ground, with the days of dual use gone and the football club in their new ground in a different part of town. The main permanent buildings are the old pavilion, the new stand and the new pavilion. There is also room for spectators to bring their own seats. Cover in wet weather is limited to the ground floor of the new stand.
All signs of the football ground-share are now gone, with the new cricket school and seating at old football ground end. It has a friendly atmosphere.
The stand above the old cricket school gives a good panoramic view. Most of the public areas have unobstructed views, with a good view from behind the bowlers' arm in the new seats by the new cricket school.

Catering and Bars:
The Old Cricket School has tea, coffee, sandwiches, pies, chocolate etc., as well as good quality snacks and light meals. There is also a bar. In the pavilion, members can buy hot drinks, sandwiches, pies, chocolate etc. The restaurant under the changing rooms offers better quality lunches and teas

Shop:
Behind old cricket school. A reasonable choice of cricket equipment, bats, clothes, books, souvenirs, bone china mugs.

General facilities
Cricket coaching facilities: Yes. Indoor cricket school.
Cricket nets: Yes. Indoor cricket school.
Other sporting or recreational facilities on the ground: No.
Facilities for hire or wider community use at the ground: Conference,

dinner and restaurant facilities.
Ticket office: Club office.
Scoreboards: Main one and small one.
Toilets: Behind pavilion and others.
Entrances: No restrictions.

Facilities and access for people with disabilities:
Usually free admission for visually impaired people. Guide dogs allowed.
New cricket school and Spenser pavilion have lifts.
Wheelchair access to the ground: Yes
Designated car parking available inside the ground: Yes. Phone first.
Viewing areas for people using wheelchairs: Yes. Designated areas.
Ramps to provide easy access to bars and refreshment outlets: Yes.
Toilets: Behind pavilion.

Travel:
Car parking: Some at ground including places reserved for the disabled.
Also street parking.
Nearest station: Northampton.
Buses: 3,7,11 and 14. Information: 01604-755155
Tourist information: Northampton Visitor Centre, Mr Grant's House, 10, St
Giles Square, NN1 1DA. Tel: 01604-622677. Fax: 01604-604180.

Road directions:
Ground is north east of town centre. From A45, at junction with A428 and
A5095, take A5095 (Rushmere Rd). Turn left onto Wellingborough Rd
(A4500), and Wantage Rd is first on right. From town centre, take
Wellingborough Rd (A4500), then as above. From M1, take junction 15,
then A508, which becomes A45, then as above.

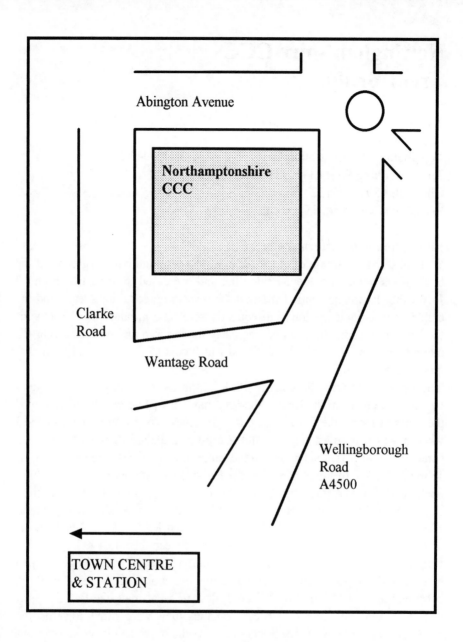

Abington Avenue

Northamptonshire CCC

Clarke
Road

Wantage Road

Wellingborough
Road
A4500

TOWN CENTRE
& STATION

Nottinghamshire CCC
Trent Bridge

Address: Trent Bridge, Bridgford Road, Nottingham, NG2 6AG
Capacity: 14,000
Telephone: 0115-982-3000   **Fax:** 0115-945-5730
Ticket booking line: 0115-981 7005
Clubcall: 0891-525152
Website: www.trentbridge.co.uk

Description and Historical Comment:
William Clarke, captain of the All-Eleven in 1846, laid out the ground at the back of his home, the Trent Bridge Inn and organised the first match on 10 July 1838. It was not until 1881 that the owners agreed a long lease and the club finally bought the inn (subsequently sold) and ground in 1919. One of the best grounds in the country, regularly modernised and now featuring the magnificent new Radcliffe Road Stand which cost £7.2 million and opened in mid summer1998.

Nottinghamshire were founded in 1859 and in the early days of the County Championship from 1873 when the least number of lost matches determined the order of merit, the County won it eight times. They won it again in 1889 when a win was given a point and a draw a half and their sides included some of the most famous names in the game. Besides Clarke, George Parr hit so many sixes into the elm tree on the leg side that it was named after him. Richard Daft was a fine batsman and his book *Kings of Cricket* is a classic.

Arthur Shrewsbury was regarded by WG as the best of all; George Gunn scored over 30,000 runs, with Wass bowling fast leg breaks and Hallam off breaks they virtually won the championship between them in 1907.

Harold Larwood emerged in 1925 and together with Voce helped Nottinghamshire to become a leading team without actually winning anything between the wars. After World War II, despite a batsman like Reg Simpson and Australian all-rounder Bruce Dooland, they were often towards the bottom of the table. Sir Gary Sobers came as the overseas player in 1968 but never really settled to county cricket and it was not until the arrival of Sir Richard Hadlee and Clive Rice, assisted by the mercurial Derek Randall that the championship was won again in 1981 and a Nat West trophy in 1987.

Views from the Boundary:
Members areas: *Pavilion, Hound Road stand, Larwood & Voce stand.*

The pavilion was built in 1886, designed by H.M. Townsend of Peterborough, has been modernised and extended but retains much of its original character.

The old Radcliffe Road Stand had happy memories for Nottinghamshire regulars who loved their cricket and the traditions of the club. It was much more popular than the Fox or even the famous Parr, with elevated views behind the bowler's arm and above all a friendly place where opposition supporters were welcomed and felt involved as part of the cricket scene.

It was more easily forgotten that a good view of the cricket and the scoreboard was not always possible in the lower tier but it was the place to be in bad weather.

While recognising the need for improvements in facilities and buildings the key task for developers is to retain as much of the essential character of the place and this has been achieved in the New Stand. It has retained several of the Victorian and Edwardian features – grey slate, clay tiles and red brick of the local area are all in keeping with a prestigious cricket ground.

Excellent viewing, residential cricket school, gymnasium, sports injury clinic and a media centre that even the press are impressed with, is an outstanding success. Let's hope it's a place where the next generation of Nottinghamshire supporters can sit in the sun and enjoy their cricket.

It holds 4,500 and has unobstructed views with three tiers and now dominates the ground. The other stands offer generally good views and some covered areas.

Catering and bars:
A choice of different places within the ground, some for members only and others not always easy to find. Harry's Bar (above the ticket office) is good value with a bar, hot and cold lunches, choice of desserts and sandwiches, but not much room. The Pavilion is for members and besides a bar, disappointingly only has chicken and chips and sandwiches but three course lunches are available in the Derek Randall Banqueting Suite.

A pass out is required for the Larwood and Voce Tavern and bar snacks, bacon and sausage baps, jacket potatoes but nothing else for vegetarians.

Strong recommendations for the new Portuguese owners of the Trent Bridge Café for so long the dreariest of greasy spoon eateries. Lunch time specials include chicken, omelettes and pies and a selection of filled baguettes, sandwiches, salads and jacket potatoes. There is plenty of egg, bangers and bacon, roast beef, steak and chips and even more interesting, soup, pate and lasagne and the usual beverages; prices are said to be very competitive. Mike and Ernesto Santos's enterprise is just what is needed on cricket grounds to much improve the image and the quality of sporting venue catering and we wish them every success.
The Trent Bridge Inn and Trent Bridge House are also by the ground.

Shop:
By William Clarke stand. It has some books, souvenirs, a good choice of clothing and cricket equipment. Further information is on the club's website.

Museum:
In the pavilion, but not open during lunch and tea - used for players meals. No admission charge, it features photos, cartoons, scorecards, a map showing birthplaces of Nottinghamshire players in the county. Collection of bats, other souvenirs, cups etc. Worth a visit during the rain or a dull period of play.

General facilities:
Cricket coaching facilities: All year round.
Cricket nets: Yes. All year round
Other sporting or recreational facilities on the ground: Squash club
Facilities for hire or wider community use at the ground: Banqueting and conference facilities.
Ticket office: By Dixon Gate (main entrance).
Scoreboards: Main scoreboard very clear. Small one on opposite side.
Toilets: All parts of the ground.
Entrances: Ticket selling point on Bridgford Road by Dixon Gate.

Facilities and access for people with disabilities:
Wheelchair users half price, visually impaired free - check in advance. Radcliffe Road stand has lifts to all levels.

Wheelchair access to the ground: Yes.
Designated car parking available inside the ground: Yes.
Viewing areas inside the ground for people using wheelchairs: Yes.
Designated areas: William Clarke stand, Hound Road stand - lower and upper (access via lift).
Ramps to provide easy access to bars and refreshment outlets: Yes.
Toilets: At least 3.

Travel:
Car parking: Some at Nottingham Forest FC. Street parking controlled. Limited at ground. Additional parking provided for big matches. City car park information: 0115-915 6830.
Nearest station: Nottingham
Buses: 8, 12, 90. Information: 0115-950-3665
Tourist information: Nottingham TIC 1-4 Smithy Row NG1 2BY.
Tel: 0115-925-5330. Fax: 0115-915-5323

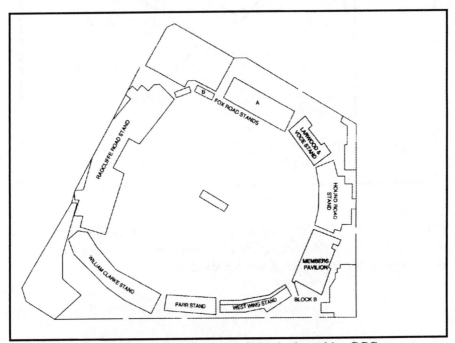

Trent Bridge plan courtesy of Nottinghamshire CCC

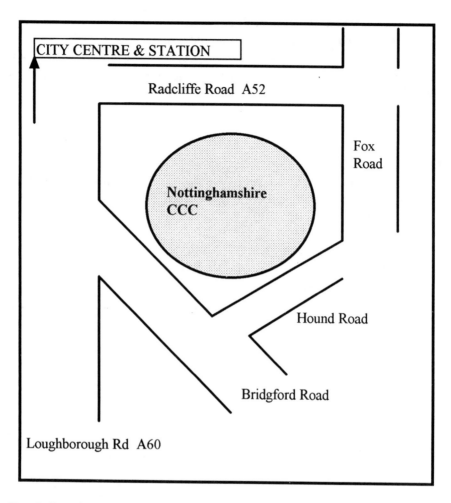

Road directions:
Near junction of A52 and A60, across Trent Bridge from city centre. Well signposted. Junction 25 from M1. Near Nottingham Forest and Notts County football grounds - traffic congestion on match days.

The museum at Trent Bridge (PDL)

The new Radcliffe Road stand, with Kwik cricket being enjoyed
at lunch time. (PDL)

65

Somerset CCC
The Clerical Medical County Ground - Taunton

Address: The Clerical Medical County Ground, St. James Street, Taunton, Somerset, TA1 1JT
Capacity: 6,000
Telephone: 01823-272946   **Fax:** 01823-332395
Ticket Office: As above
Marketing Department: 01823-337598 **Club shop:** 01823-337597
Centre of cricketing excellence: 01823-352266
Rapid Cricketline: 0930-161213

Description and Historical Comment:
Somerset were formed in 1875 and The County Ground at Taunton featured its first match against Hampshire in August 1882, the home team winning by five wickets, their only victory of the season. St. James's is the best known of three spires overlooking the ancient Ridley Stand.

Taunton CC and the Somerset Stragglers both have small separate pavilions for their members.

Taunton's history is associated with great personalities, enterprising players and achieving the unexpected rather than winning titles. In 1900 Sammy Woods led Somerset to famous victories against Yorkshire when the Tykes were beating everyone else.

In 1925 in the same match Hobbs equalled and overtook Grace's record of 126 centuries at Taunton.

In 1935, 21 year old Harold Gimblett, batting at eight in his first county match hit 123 in sixty three minutes.

Inspired by Botham, (80 sixes in 1985) Richards and Garner, Somerset won the Gillette Cup and Sunday League in 1979 and two Benson and Hedges Finals; and were extremely exciting to watch in one day cricket. However, they are still one of only four counties who have never won the county championship.

Views from the Boundary:

Members' areas: *Colin Atkinson Pavilion, Old Pavilion, Ridley stand and Members' enclosures at car park end and by old indoor school.*

The ground is rapidly changing with the Atkinson Pavilion; executive suites, vice presidents stand and the new two tier Ian Botham Stand with multi media centre and hospitality boxes on the top floor.

Seating for members is within pavilions behind the bowlers' arm and the public sit on green bucket seats on the other two sides, with the view from the River End across to the churches the most attractive.

Taunton is part of the life of the city with people popping in from shopping or straight from work to watch the cricket. Inside the pavilion is smart and comfortable with a good bar and dining facilities with bucket seats in front with easy access for refreshment while watching the game.

The view from the pavilion is fine leg/long off and much straighter from the Botham Stands and although the Old Pavilion and Ridley Road Stands are clearly a shrine for some they seem gloomy and uncongenial and I can't get away from them quickly enough.

The River Stand with long bench seats is shady but a bit reminiscent of an old football stadium and the limes on the east side give more cover on what is often a quiet area of the ground.

Catering and Bars:

Colin Atkinson Pavilion and Botham stand both offer good and comfortable access to bars and refreshment and are the best places on the ground. The Old Pavilion and Ridley Road Stand have snacks and a cafeteria service where there are always queues for homely looking hot food or fresh salads and lots of apple pie and custard. Stragglers and Taunton CC are reported to be full of good cricket talk and hospitable to their members; the former certainly will be when the reach their centenary in the millennium.

For the general public, there is a fast food, snacks and sandwich bar which is pretty ordinary but the bacon butties are good and if you spill your tea they will probably replace it free of charge. Otherwise cider and more snacks available in the corner next to the River Stand .

Shop:
The County shop is well appointed and besides cricket merchandise includes books and magazines as well as newspapers which are not always available on cricket grounds.

Museum:
The museum in a converted barn is exceptional with many interesting Somerset photographs, scorecards and numerous memorabilia providing a comprehensive history of the players, great matches and achievements of the club. Open during matches.

General facilities:
Cricket coaching facilities: Yes. Indoor school.
Cricket nets: Yes.
Other sporting or recreational facilities on the ground: No.
Facilities for hire or wider community use at the ground: Rooms for wedding receptions, dinners, meetings etc.
Ticket office: Club office.
Scoreboards: One by Colin Atkinson pavilion, other by public seating.
Toilets: Very good modern ones at the Priory Bridge Road end including facilities for disabled people. Ancient ones hidden away in other parts of the ground in need of upgrading.

Facilities and access for people with disabilities:
Reduced admission for visually impaired and wheelchair users - depends on match. Check with club. Group bookings possible for championship matches - book in advance. Commentary when members available.
Wheelchair access to the ground: Yes.
Designated car parking available inside the ground: Yes.
Viewing areas for people using wheelchairs: Yes. Designated areas.
Match commentaries for visually handicapped people: Yes (on request).
Ramps to provide easy access to bars and refreshment outlets: At most.

Travel:
Car parking: Vice President members and people with disabilities only at ground. Local car parks, and at Rugby Ground.
Nearest station: Taunton.

Buses: Shuttle 1 or 2 to Tone River Bridge. Very near bus station. Information: 01823-272033.
Tourist information: Taunton TIC, Paul Street, Taunton, TA1 3XZ. 01823-336344. Fax: 01823-340308.

Road directions:
Well sign posted from the M5. Take junction 25, A358 and join A38 towards town centre. At roundabout take Priory Avenue (A3038), straight over next roundabout, into Priory Bridge Road, and ground is on left.

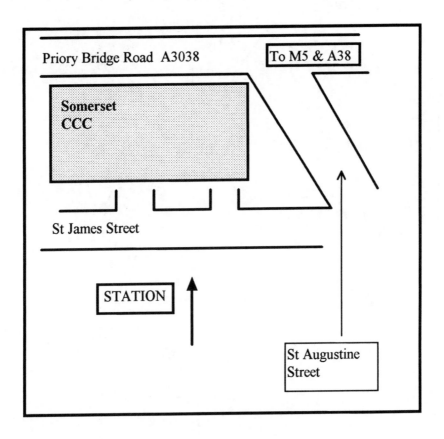

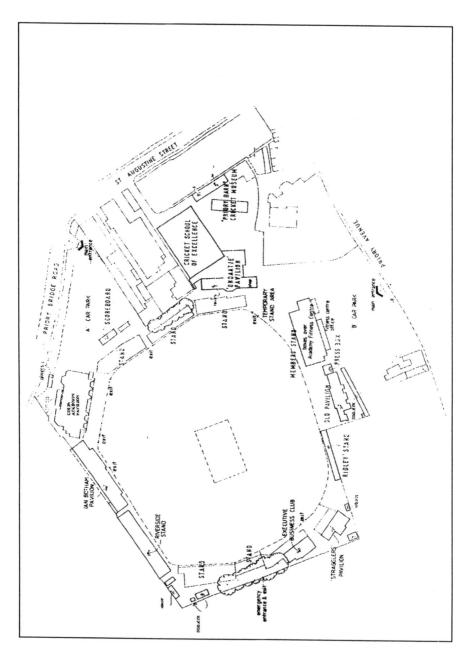

The Clerical Medical County Ground plan courtesy of Somerset CCC

70

CRICKET MEMORABILIA SOCIETY

Founded in April 1987

Over 800 members worldwide

Annual Subscription: £10
Senior citizens: £6
Youth(under 18): £2
Overseas airmail: £5 extra

For further information,
write to:
Mr T. Sheldon
29, Highclere Road
Crumpsall,
Manchester M8 4WH

A Society for Collectors

Surrey CCC
The Fosters' Oval

Address: The Oval, Kennington, London, SE11 5SS
Capacity: 17,000
Telephone: 0171-582-6660   **Fax:** 0171-735-7769
Ticket office: 0171-582-7764.   **Fax:** 0171-793-7520
Website: www.surreyccc.co.uk
The Fosters' Oval Shop: 0171-820-1866. **Fax:** 0171-735-7769
Ken Barrington Cricket Centre (The Fosters' Oval): As above.
Surrey County Cricket Centre (Guildford): 01483-598880
Fax: 01483-598881

Description and historical comment:
Although Lord's is generally regarded as the principal Test ground in London, Surrey CCC dates from 1845 and featured its first championship game against Sussex in 1873. More important and largely due to its imaginative and enterprising secretary C.W. Alcock, the ground staged the first Test match against Australia in 1880 when Grace scored 152 not out. The ground has traditionally always staged the final Test in the series and the famous pavilion was built in 1896 designed by A. Muirhead who was also responsible for the Old Trafford pavilion. It also staged the F.A. Cup Final in the nineteenth century and senior amateur football into the 1950s.
Oval Test matches are legendary including Jessop's fabulous 104 followed by the Hirst and Rhodes "we'll get 'em in singles" 15 runs to win the match in 1902; Hutton's famous 364 in 1938, Bradman's dismissal for a duck on his last appearance in 1948 and Viv Richards' magnificent 291 in 1976.
But rather more than Lord's for Middlesex, The Oval is essentially the home of Surrey CCC and particularly their two periods of extraordinary dominance in the championship with nine titles between 1880 and 1900 and seven consecutive victories in the 1950s. The first period belonged to the trilogy of fast bowlers, George Lohmann, Tom Richardson and Bill Lockwood with Bobby Abel the outstanding batsman.
The second, led by the dynamic Stuart Surridge, included the Bedser twins, Peter May, young Ken Barrington, Laker, Lock and Loader. In the 'middle years' Jack Hobbs was the greatest name of all, scorer of 61,237 runs and

197 centuries and a master batsman. Hayward, Sandham, Jardine, Fender were heavy scorers and strong personalities and more recently John Edrich, Micky Stewart and his son Alec, the present England captain have led the way but still no championship since the 1950s.

Views from the Boundary:
Members areas: *Pavilion*

The gas holders (are they up or down?), festooned council flats where the roofs and balconies sometimes provide an unoffical view of big matches and Archbishop Tenison school are the enduring features of essentially the Londoners ground. The ground is much changed but the grand pavilion looks little different with improvements to the top tier and major development to the stands on either side with hospitality boxes, new dressing rooms and smart modernisation. Look out for the new clock.

Test Match tickets require booking as soon as details are available. Cricket followers like The Oval so much that there is a waiting list for the top level of membership which includes Test Match tickets and you have to graduate through the second level to qualify for consideration.

Most areas offer unrestricted views, but with the size of the Oval, you can be quite far from the action if your seat is on one side and the wicket on the far side of the square. The Lock & Laker and Fender stands offer some cover. The views from the lower part of the Lock & Laker stand is slightly restricted due to roof pillars.

Catering and Bars:
A wide range of catering outlets on big match days with sit down lunches for members in the Banqueting Suite and for corporate guests in the numerous hospitality boxes. The bar at the rear of the Tavern is a popular meeting place and the Mound Bar by the Lock and Laker has sandwiches and light refreshments. There are plenty of fast food outlets and often a baguette bar all round the ground

Shop:
By Hobbs gate. Clothing, good selection of books and some videos. Also has pictures, postcards and souvenirs.

Museum:
There is surprisingly no official museum but the pavilion contains many very interesting paintings and portraits of famous players and teams in the Long Room and round the interior which contribute a great deal to the history and atmosphere of the building. The library was opened in 1980 to celebrate the centenary of the first Test Match and it contains numerous cricket books, old Surrey yearbooks and copies of Wisden.

General facilities:
Cricket coaching facilities: Yes.
Cricket nets: Ken Barrington Cricket Centre.
Other sporting or recreational facilities on the ground: Health club.
Facilities for hire or wider community use at the ground: Conference rooms, banqueting facilities etc.
Other sporting recreational / leisure activities: Occasional use - Australian rules football, baseball.
Ticket office: By Hobbs gate.
Scoreboards: Electronic by Bedser stand. Manual by Peter May enclosure.
Toilets: In all areas of the ground.
Entrances: No restrictions.

Facilities and access for people with disabilities:
No reduced admission. Guide dogs allowed.
Wheelchair access to the ground: Yes.
Designated car parking available inside the ground: Yes.
Viewing areas for people using wheelchairs: Yes. Designated areas.
Ramps to provide easy access to bars and refreshment outlets: Yes.
Toilets: By health and fitness club.

Travel:
Car parking: None at ground except for disabled - check with club. Street parking very limited, and up to 0.5 miles from Ground.
Nearest station: The Oval (London Underground) and Vauxhall
Buses: 36 and 185. Information: 0171-222-1234
Tourist information: 0839-123456 (premium rate). Tourist information centres at Victoria station and Liverpool St station.

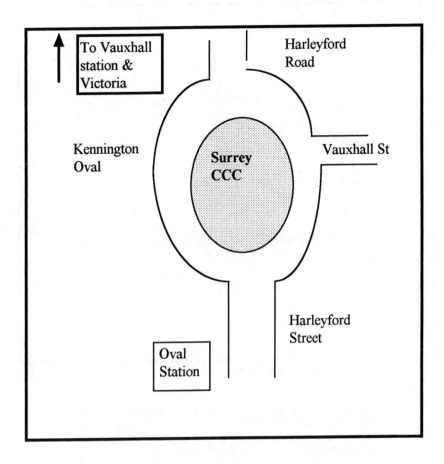

Road directions
The ground is just south of Vauxhall Bridge on the A202, Vauxhall Road. It is also by the junction of the A3 and A23. The ground is on the A3 (Kennington Park Road) is about a mile south of Elephant and Castle. Look out for the Oval station.

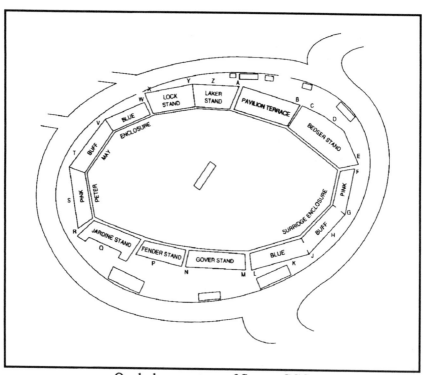

Oval plan courtesy of Surrey CCC

Musical entertainment - day night match at The Oval (PDL)

Television and the lights at Hove (PDL)

"Keep Off" at Taunton (RO)

Sussex CCC
Hove - County Ground

Address: County Ground, Eaton Road, Hove, East Sussex, BN3 3AN
Capacity: 5,000
Telephone: 01273-827100. **Fax:** 01273-771549
Ticket office: As above
Membership hotline: 01273-207208
Youth Development Office: 01273-735143
Information service & scores: 0336-500131. **Faxback:** 0336-421701.

Description and Historical Comment:
With views of blocks of flats and a featureless collection of buildings around the pavilion there is not much architecturally to commend Hove. But for history and nostalgia and particularly "the fret" and "the slope" there are still some who are pleased to hear that Sussex intend to stay there. There are fond memories of Ranji, C.B. Fry, Duleep, Maurice Tate, the Gilligans, the Parks and the Langridges and more recent memories of David Sheppard, the former Bishop of Liverpool, Ted Dexter, John Snow and Tony Greig.

Sussex cricket headquarters has been at Eaton Road since 1872 with the first county match a rain ruined draw against Gloucestershire. After the glory days of John Wisden (founder of the Almanack) and Lilleywhite towards the end of the nineteenth century Sussex generally found themselves near the bottom of the table. The great Australian W.I. Murdoch had captained the side, handed over to Ranji in 1899 and for a few years they were immensely strong in batting but short of top class bowling. Ranji and Fry were the great stars and for eight seasons, from 1896-1904 scored at will. But, with their subsequent departure, Sussex were once again a struggling side. In 1911 the Nottinghamshire batsman Ted Alletson scored a still unbelievable 189 in 90 minutes, the last 142 coming in 40 minutes and including 34 in one over off Killick.

Between the wars, Maurice Tate, with 2,784 wickets was among the best two or three in the country; Ranji's nephew Duleep was a phenomenal batsman who scored 7,791 runs between 1929-31 and his 333 against Northamptonshire in 1930 remains the highest score on the ground. Since World War II Sussex have continued to struggle to develop a championship winning team, but Ted Dexter led them to victories in the first two Gillette Cup final in 1963 and 1964. They won it again in 1978 and a Nat West Trophy in 1986.

Views from the boundary:
Members areas: *Pavilion, deck chairs and benches.*

Sussex is the oldest club in the country and entrance is past the Sussex Cricketer public house through the famous Tate Gates from Eaton Road. The George Cox memorial garden has early season blossom and the main scoreboard and clock tower are on the East side.
The pavilion was built in the 1880s with the upper tier rebuilt in 1961 and is architecturally undistinguished and it is almost impossible to find your way around without advice. Although the view is from square leg spectators feel close to the play and much more involved with the scene than at many other grounds. Internally despite, or perhaps because of, a sense of disorientation it is nice to come cross an old picture or scorecard of a memorable match.
Sussex have recently received planning approval to install permanent floodlights to be used on 20 days in the summer and be turned off by 11 p.m. Incongruous but if they decide to stay at Hove a possible money spinner. There are many priorities for modernisation and redevelopment.
For a sunny day, the deck chairs are very tempting, but do not offer the best view. A more panoramic view from the Arthur Gilligan stand by the main entrance. The public seats between the main entrance and pavilion offer an unrestricted view. Uncovered temporary seating provided for big matches at north end and by scoreboard.

Catering and bars:
Meals provided in the restaurant (Ted Dexter Room) for members. Sandwiches, tea, coffee and a bar also available in the pavilion. By the pavilion, try the fish and chips, and by the scoreboard, jacket potatoes are available along with other snacks. There is also the pub "The Sussex Cricketer" by main entrance.

Shop:
By main entrance. There is a good selection of cricket equipment, souvenirs, clothing, books and some videos / tapes.

Museum:
None, but there is a library which is an excellent source of information about Sussex CCC.

General facilities:
Cricket coaching facilities: All year round. Indoor cricket school.
Cricket nets: All year round. Indoor cricket school.
Other sporting or recreational facilities on the ground: No
Facilities for hire or wider community use at the ground: Dining and conference facilities
Other: Mother and Baby room in indoor cricket school.
Ticket office: By pavilion
Scoreboards: Main scoreboard opposite pavilion.
Toilets: Behind deck-chair area and in other areas of the ground.
Entrances: Both ends of the ground.

Facilities and access for people with disabilities:
No reduced admission for visually impaired people except in pre-booked groups. Guide dogs allowed.
Wheelchair access to the ground: Yes
Designated car parking available inside the ground: Yes.
Viewing areas for people using wheelchairs: Yes. No specific area, but flat areas in various parts of the ground.
Ramps to provide easy access to bars and refreshment outlets: No.
Toilets: In indoor cricket school.

Travel:
Car parking: Some for members at ground. Street parking - unrestricted, but can be very busy. Local car parks.
Nearest station: Hove. Brighton station is less than 1 mile away.
Buses: 7and 7a from Hove and Brighton stations.
Information: 01273-700406.
Tourist information: Hove TIC, Church Road, BN3 3BQ. 01273-292589.

Road directions:
A23 towards Brighton. Before reaching town, follow signs for A27, Hove/Worthing. Keep in left hand lane following signs to Hove. At roundabout, take second exit to Brighton (Dyke Rd). Turn right into Woodland Drive, and left into Shirley Drive This becomes The Drive. Turn left into Eaton Road, and ground is on left.
Driving along the sea front, from Brighton Town Centre, pass West Pier (closed) and turn right up Grand Avenue. Take second right into Eaton Road, and ground is on left.

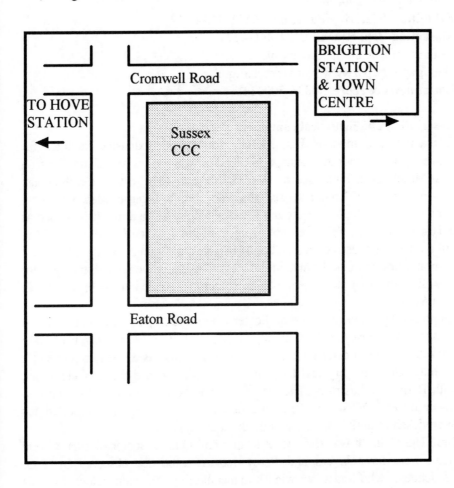

Warwickshire CCC
Edgbaston - County Ground

Address: Edgbaston Road, Edgbaston, Birmingham, BS 7 QU
Capacity: 20,000
Telephone: 0121-446-4422   **Fax:** 0121-446-4544
Ticket office: 0121-446-5506
Club shop: 0121-446-4787
Exhibitions/Catering/Functions: 0121-440-0747
Marketing Department: 0121-446-4777
E-mail: info@warwickccc.org.uk.
Web page: http://www.warwickccc.org.uk
Latest news & scores: 0336-500111

Description and historical comment:
Edgbaston is a modern Test Match ground with extensive facilities for members and corporate guests, and plenty of attractions and distractions on Test Match days. First used by Warwickshire in 1894, it staged a three day Test match in 1902 against Australia who, despite being bowled out for 36 in an hour and a half by Hirst and Rhodes, held on for a draw. It was used as a Test venue until 1929, but not again until 1957, when Cowdrey and May put on their famous record stand of 411 to save the game. Having taken 7 for 49 in the first innings, Ramadhin bowled 98 overs in the second, taking 2 for 179 and delivering more balls than any other in a single innings or in a whole Test Match.

Captained by 22 year old Frank Foster who scored 1,459 runs and took 124 wickets W Warwickshire's championship victory in 1911 astonished the cricketing world. Foster's remarkable six year career is a legend of cricket; a dashing batsman, very fast left arm bowler who opened the England attack with Barnes in Australia. The war came, and he was severely disabled in a motor cycle accident in 1915. His famous 'double' was not repeated for Warwickshire until Tom Cartwright did it in 1962.

Jim 'Tiger' Smith was the wicket keeper and Quaife, scorer of over 35,000 runs, were key players and Percy Jeeves, a bowler observed by P.G. Wodehouse, who was a Warwickshire member, was the name adopted for his fictional butler. Between the wars R.E.S. Wyatt with 85 hundreds and 40

Test Matches, including 16 as captain, was an outstanding leader and in 1951 Tom Dollery aided by Eric Hollies led Warwickshire to their second title. Hollies is probably best known for depriving Sir Donald Bradman of a Test average of a hundred, but he took 2,201 wickets for his county. Dollery was succeeded by MJK Smith, a prolific scorer and brilliant close catcher leading to a Gillette Cup victory in 1966.

Views from the Boundary:
Members' areas: *Pavilion, William Ansell stand, Tom Dollery stand, Leslie Deakin stand, RV Ryder stand (lower).*

An extraordinary architectural mishmash of buildings, Edgbaston is a major stadium on big occasions, but despite outstanding team performances in the 1990s with wide open spaces of terrace embankment it is difficult to create the right atmosphere for County cricket.

The original, but much altered pavilion is hardly visible even when the players emerge from it among the West Wing stand and Executive Suites in that part of the ground. Ryder was an eminent secretary around 1900 but it was the enterprising Supporter's Association in the 1950s who enabled the club to progress numerous ground improvements.

The William Ansell Stand was built in the 1950's and more recently Priory and Raglan with additional hospitality suites and the Barnes, Hollies (or Rea Bank), and Deakins stands are named after eminent Warwickshire officials or players. Viewing is good from most parts of the ground with open tiered seating at the City End and in front of the main stands at the Pavilion End.

Some Edgbaston Test Match visitors have ruined everyone else's pleasure by chanting, and offensively disturbing others in the Rea Bank Stand. In 1998, the County employed an outside security firm which added to a tense atmosphere, and bag searching for beer cans and bottles of wine seems an unfair penalty for ordinary people, particularly as the bars remained open.

Warwickshire are understandably very concerned, have reviewed the situation and reported their findings to the ECB. There will be alcohol restrictions again this year on admission to the ground this is no inconvenience to members, hospitality guests and lager louts. A combination of pre-booking, high prices, and rowdyism must deter parents and children from attending big games. The ECB can be pleased at their marketing success for corporate hospitality but they must now concentrate on the grass roots interests of the game. What about a family stand? What about a pay on the day allocation for local cricket clubs?

Catering and bars:
Warwickshire have high standard catering and hospitality facilities with many catering outlets all round the ground on Test Match occasions. These are inevitably in the fast food, hamburgers, chicken and chips range. Lunch boxes are also available on the ground. There are plenty of members' bars in the stands and around the ground all named after fielding positions. Hot and cold food for members for county matches, but what is available for the public in the Press Box Stand and in the Long On and Third Man bars on these occasions depends on the number of spectators on the ground.

Shop:
The large shop has a range of fashion tops, sporting merchandise and Bears Kids kit, memorabilia, and with some 250 cricket titles and audio tapes can consider itself to be the best specialist cricket bookshop in the Midlands; on a cricket ground it is the best in the country comparable to Lord's. See the club's website for further information. There was also a good second hand book stall near the Edgbaston Road entrance.

Museum:
There is a good museum which was curiously open for members only on the Friday of last year's Test Match.

General facilities:
Cricket coaching facilities: Yes. Juniors only in summer, juniors, adults & clubs in winter.
Cricket nets: Yes. Summer: youth teams. Juniors, adults & clubs in winter
Other sporting or recreational facilities on the ground: No
Facilities for hire or wider community use at the ground: Function rooms for weddings, conferences, dinners etc.
Ticket office: Club offices.
Scoreboards: One by Stanley Barnes stand, one by Ryder stand.
Toilets: There are ample toilet facilities, but for the public the up to date facilities at the Pavilion End are best, avoid the ancient brick urinals near the main public stands. Facilities for disabled people in the main toilet areas

Facilities and access for people with disabilities:
The stewards are very helpful. Except for internationals there is reduced free admission for wheelchair users and visually impaired people. There is also reduced rate membership including companions, reflecting a particularly positive attitude. Guide dogs are allowed.
Designated car parking available inside the ground: Yes.
Viewing areas for people using wheelchairs: Yes. Designated areas in front of the Thwaites scoreboard.
Ramps to provide easy access to bars and refreshment outlets: No - lift access to some areas.

Travel:
Car parking: Some for members at ground. Usually parking in Calthorpe Park, and local car parks. Parking on Test Match days is best booked in advance or there are additional signed car parking areas within reasonable walking distance of the ground.
Nearest station: Birmingham New Street (1 mile).
Buses: 45 & 47 from city centre (Corporation Street).
Information: 0121-200-2700.
Tourist information: Birmingham Convention & Visitor Bureau, 2, City Arcade, B2 4TX. 0121-643-2514. Fax: 0121-616-1038.

Road directions:
From city centre, take A441 south, turn left into Edgbaston Road (B4217), and ground is on right. Well sign posted from M6. Use ring road to link up with A441 from other directions.
MS (J4) follow A38 through Selly Oak and then follow yellow AA signs to Edgbaston.
M6 (J6) follow A38 through city centre and after 1.5 miles go left at traffic lights into Priory Road. Cross Pershore Road traffic lights and entrance off Edgbaston Road.

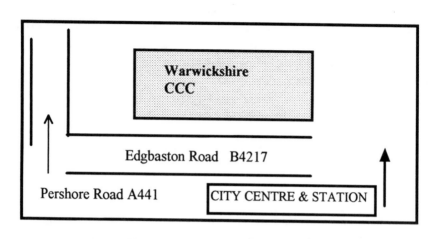

Edgbaston Road   B4217

Pershore Road A441

CITY CENTRE & STATION

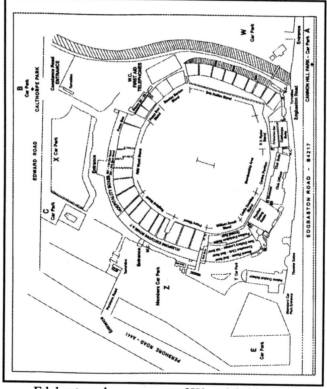

Edgbaston plan courtesy of Warwickshire CCC

86

Cricket Lore

Worcestershire CCC
New Road - County Ground

Address: County Ground, New Road, Worcester, WR2 4QQ
Capacity: 4,500
Telephone: 01905-748474   **Fax:** 01905-748005
Ticket office: 01905-422694
Cricket Suite Caterers: 01905-423561 or 01905-420274 (Tel/fax)
Supporters Association: 01905-424739
Rapid Cricketline: 0930-161217

Description and Historical Comment:
The County Ground at New Road is one of the most charming and delightful cricket grounds, bounded by the Severn, overlooked by the14[th] century cathedral, All Saints Church and St. Andrews Tower and Spire or "the glover's needle". The first match was on 4 May 1899 against a Yorkshire side that included Hirst and Rhodes and won a close game by seven runs. Sir Donald Bradman enjoyed opening his accounts here with three double centuries and a final 107 on his four visits.

In the early days, seven Foster brothers played for the county, all of them considerable cricketers, with R. E. Foster an outstanding batsman who scored 287 against Australia at Sydney in 1903-4. Worcestershire achieved little success before the first World War or between the wars although Fred Root's in-swing dominated the second period with outstanding performances. In his final season, aged 41 he took 9 for 23 against Lancashire, the best ever performance by a Worcestershire bowler

C.F. Walters was good enough to score a century for England and captained them on one occasion but it was bowlers such Dick Howarth, Roly Jenkins, an exceptional leg spinner and above all fast bowler Reg Perks who held the stage. Perks regularly took 100 wickets and was unlucky to be competing with Sir Alec Bedser, as well as Truman and Statham for an England place.

For many years a Cinderella, the County's first moment of glory came in 1964 when Don Kenyon with ten wins in the last eleven led them to the championship Tom Graveney had by then qualified for Worcestershire and together with the Richardson brothers, Martin Horton, Flavell and Coldwell leading the attack, they became a top side. Basil D'Olivera and subsequently

Glenn Turner and Graeme Hick came in helped towards three more championships in 1965, 1974 and 1988 plus a B & H Cup in 1991 and Nat West Trophy in 1995.

Views from the Boundary:
Members areas: *Pavilion, New Road stand.*

New Road is often flooded and features aquatic activities, but despite this the pavilion that was completed in 1898 looks much the same today. The Ladies Pavilion opened in 1956 and maintains a well deserved reputation for lemon or chocolate sponge and much else at knock down prices and all are welcome onwards from 3 p.m. There is also a interesting collection of old Wisdens and other cricket books for a good browse round when its raining.
Viewing is good from all around the ground. One of the pleasures is ringing the changes from the Diglis Road, to side on facing the three spires, or across to the ancient pavilion or sitting under the chestnuts on a hot day.
The congenial atmosphere at New Road amply compensates for wooden bench seating and the only covered seating for members is in the gloomy New Road stand. It is open stand bucket seating all round the ground and the pleasures are in the setting and indefinable atmosphere.
There is an executive suite on the site of the former Supporters Association's offices and these enthusiastic and extremely hard working supporters are now in offices with the club's marketing department. The Worcester Supporters Association play a major part in the County's cricket and this is reflected in the positive and friendly attitudes of staff at the ground.

Catering and Bars:
Well organised and imaginative catering in the pavilion, with a restaurant in the cricket suite; bar meals and snacks based on chicken, scampi, steak and fried fish with plenty of chips in a basket. Worth getting in before the lunch interval otherwise its a queuing system, with time for a drink at the excellent bar. Much less enticing fare in the public areas, beside the main scoreboard from a mobile and featuring lukewarm, rather flaky pasties, and mainly white bread sandwiches. There are sandwiches and pork pies at the kiosk just inside the ground but why don't they do raspberries and cream and other soft fruits in a place like Worcester? Perhaps its something for Lannies ices to think about.

Shops:
The new shop has replaced the Severn Bar and like others it is just like going into a small sports merchandise section in a general store, but the shirts, sweaters and track suits have a Worcestershire logo on them. No books or other items of cricket interest; a few are to be found in the minute space available to the ladies from the Supporters Association who seem to be squeezed out a bit more every year. As they have an enclosed kiosk there is no browsing space and you have to know what you want before you arrive at the window.

Museum:
There is no museum but perhaps one might find itself into the plan for a Basil D'Olivera Cricket Centre.

General facilities:
Cricket coaching facilities: No.
Cricket nets: No.
Other sporting or recreational facilities on the ground: No.
Facilities for hire or wider community use at the ground: Yes.
Ticket office: Club office.
Public address system: Public address is generally audible and reliable including information about ground facilities and interval scores from other grounds although these would benefit from a bit more detail about exceptional bowling and batting performances.
Scoreboards: Attractive, traditional scoreboards are easy to read with the main Diglis Road board housed under pitched roofs and the other giving the total score, batsmen's scores with one space for the bowler.
Toilets: Good amenities in the pavilion and modern toilet and washing facilities adjacent to the New Road entrance and the club shop. Rather more rudimentary standards hidden away behind the Ladies Pavilion and the main scoreboard.

Facilities and access for people with disabilities:
Guide dogs are allowed. No reduced admission, but companions free for some matches.
Wheelchair access to the ground: Yes
Designated car parking available inside the ground: Yes. 9 spaces in front

of main scoreboard.
Viewing areas for people using wheelchairs: Yes. Designated areas.
Ramps to provide easy access to bars and refreshment outlets: Yes.
Toilets: Adjacent to New Road entrance and club shop.

Travel:
Car parking: Ground: members with season passes only. Sundays:
Christopher Whitehead school - free for car park pass holders, £1.50 for
others. NCP car parks in city centre or on left beside river.
Nearest station: Worcester (Foregate St)
Buses: Any that go to St John's. 44, 23,24,25,26,33, 144 (Sundays only and
others. Information: 0345-125436
Tourist information: Worcester TIC, The Guildhall, High Street, WR1 2EY.
01905-726311. Fax: 01905-722481

Road directions:
AA signs for Worcester Races are prominent but follow them for the City
Centre. Take Bridge Street (A38) and go left over the bridge. For parking
adjacent to ground, go immediately left behind garage. For ground, continue
on A44, down New Road, and ground is on left.

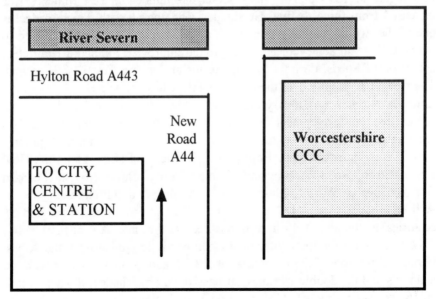

Yorkshire CCC
Headingley

Address: Headingley Cricket Ground, St Michael's Lane, Leeds,
LS6 3BU
Capacity: 15,500
Telephone: 0113-278-7394   **Fax:** 0113-278-4099
Ticket office: As above.
Rapid cricket line: 0891-567518
White Rose shop: 0113-275-3290
Website: www.yorkshireccc.org.uk
Email: cricket@yorkshireccc.org.uk

Description and Historical Comment:
For the first hundred years of cricket history, Yorkshire were pre-eminent among the counties, winning the championship thirty one times and sharing it twice, the last occasion in 1968. The headquarters of Yorkshire cricket was initially at Bramall Lane, Sheffield. Yorkshire played their first game at Headingley in 1890 and in 1899, when the number of Test Matches was increased from three to five, Headingley was chosen with Trent Bridge as one of the two additional grounds. The Yorkshire authorities have failed to match their team achievements with ground improvements and a featureless collection of Sheds are now inadequate for an historic Test Match ground. The recent uncertainty over the ground's future has not helped.
Lord Hawke was a visionary aristocrat whose ideas and principles set the context for the development of cricket in the county. Yorkshire produced a remarkable sequence of great English cricketers through the generations. From Tom Emmett, Ulyett, Bobby Peel, Rhodes and Hirst, Haig, the Hon. F.S. Jackson, Sutcliffe, Leyland, Hedley Verity, Bowes to Sir Leonard Hutton, Boycott, Wardle, Close, Truman, Appleyard and Illingworth.
Wilfred Rhodes took 4,187 wickets at 16.71, scored 39,802 runs and 58 centuries; at the age of 48 he was recalled for the final Test at the Oval in 1926, took 4 for 44 and contributed significantly to wining back the Ashes. George Hirst took 2,739 wickets at 18.72 and scored 36,323 with 60 hundreds, did the double 14 times, surpassed only by Rhodes who achieved it on 16 occasions. Sutcliffe (149 centuries) and Holmes were peerless openers

and Hedley Verity in a short but incandescent career took 1,956 wickets at 14.87 including 14 for 80 against the Australians in 1934 - the only occasion this century that England have beaten their oldest rivals at Lord's.

Sir Leonard Hutton was a supreme Test Match batsman, scorer of 41,140 runs and 129 centuries, the first professional captain of England, and the second to be knighted for his services to cricket. His career was interrupted by war and he didn't play a Test Match at Headingley until 1947 against the South Africans when he scored a hundred in difficult conditions. Geoffrey Boycott, the run machine with 48,426 runs and 151 centuries was the first to score his 100th hundred in a Test Match, and he made it at Headingley.

Sir Donald Bradman liked Headingley, scoring 334 in 1930, including 105 before lunch and 309 in a day; 304 in 1934; 103 in 1938 and 173 not out in the second innings in 1948. More recently, Botham's epic 145, followed by an inspired 8 for 42 from Willis, obliged the players to re-book their hotel rooms and England won the match.

Yorkshire's more recent history has been a combination of organisational and dressing room disharmony. the frequent turnover of captains, and apart from winning the B & H Cup in 1987 showed no sign of improvement in championship cricket.

While other teams were recruiting outstanding overseas players, Yorkshire maintained their policy of fielding a Yorkshire only team until they changed in 1991 and appointed Sachin Tendulkar as an overseas player in 1992.

Views from the boundary:
Members areas: *Pavilion, Bowling Green stand, Main stand.*

Just a few examples of great cricketing personalities and occasions make it even more difficult for outsiders to understand why Yorkshire have been unable to sustain even modest ground improvements. The main stand with its extended grey roof is dull; the pavilion accommodates the office, the press box and scorers' room with bars and catering facilities for members. Yardley and Kilburn wrote in the 1950s that "the refreshment arrangements are decidedly utilitarian", things have very little changed.

Disorderly conduct and rowdyism has been a regular feature on the Western Terrace in recent years and of considerable concern to the authorities. Although this is a complex problem by no means exclusive to Headingley, primitive ground decisions, inadequate circulation areas and vast open terraces must significantly contribute to the attitudes and behaviour of spectators and discourage family spectators.

It is good news to be able to report that Leeds Council have recently approved a £30m development scheme for both the rugby and cricket grounds. The Winter Sheds and eastern pavilion are to be replaced by a single-tier stand around to the Kirstall Lane End with another single tier stand along the Cardigan Road boundary. A media centre and museum are also included and we must hope for rapid implementation.

Most areas offer unrestricted views, but very little under cover in public areas. The Western Terrace has alcohol restrictions for international and Test Matches.

Catering and bars:

Meals for members only in main stand. Try the Winter Shed bar for a limited choice of sandwiches, drinks, tea and coffee. Baked potato and fast food vans at some matches, but in general a very limited choice at county matches for a Test match ground, though more variety is provided for Test matches. Many spectators try fish and chip or fast food shops outside the ground for something more substantial.

Shop:

The White Rose shop, which is behind the scoreboard at the Kirkstall Lane end. It has clothing, souvenirs, some cricket equipment, books, daily newspapers, chocolates and sweets.

General facilities:

Cricket coaching facilities: Indoor cricket school.

Cricket nets: Indoor cricket school.

Other sporting or recreational facilities on the ground: Rugby League and Rugby Union on the adjoining rugby ground.

Facilities for hire or wider community use at the ground: Facilities for wedding receptions, conferences, banquets etc.

Ticket office: County office.

Scoreboards: Two. Both clear.

Toilets: By county office, near Kirkstall Lane entrance and in other parts of the ground.

Facilities and access for people with disabilities:
No free admission for visually impaired people. Commentary available - book in advance. Guide dogs allowed - give a few days warning.
Wheelchair access to the ground: Yes.
Designated car parking available inside the ground: Contact club.
Viewing areas for people using wheelchairs: Yes. No specific area, but room for wheelchairs in various parts of the ground.
Ramps to provide easy access to bars and refreshment outlets: Yes.
Toilets: By county office.

Travel:
Road restrictions on match days: Streets near ground. No parking for major matches.
Car parking: Very limited at ground. Some in local streets, limited for big matches.
Nearest station: Headingley. Information: 0345-484950
Buses: 38 and 91 from station. 56,57,74,75,76. Information: 0113-245-7676
Special transport arrangements on match days: Park and ride for Test Matches
Tourist information: Gateway Yorkshire, Station Arcade, PO Box 244, LS1 1PL. 0113-242-5242. Fax: 0113-246-8246

Headingley's main stand, with a rugby floodlight in the background (PDL)

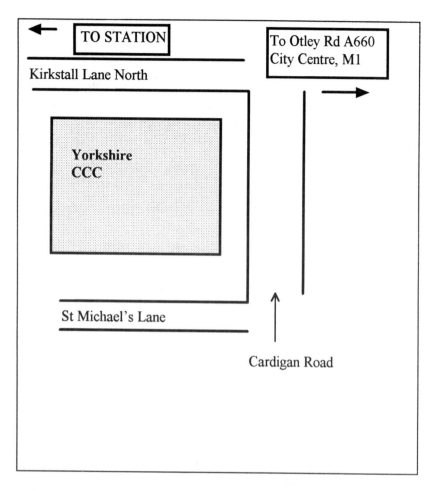

Road directions

From south, east: M1 junction 47, then M621 junction 2 A643 towards city centre. Join A58(M) and follow signs for A660 (Otley, Skipton). Join A660, which becomes Headingley Lane, then Otley Road. Turn left into Kirkstall Lane North, and ground is on left. *From west:* M62 junction 27 take M621 to junction 2, then as above.

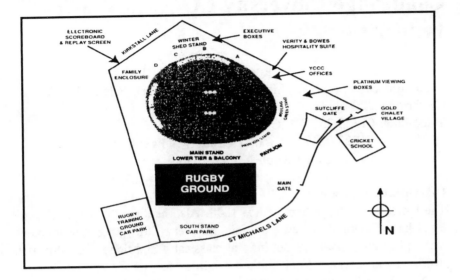

Headingley plan courtesy Yorkshire CCC

Cambridge University CC
Fenner's

Ground address: Mortimer Road, Cambridge CB1 2EL.
Club address: Prof. K. Siddle (Hon. Treasurer), Churchill College, Cambridge CB3 0DS
Telephone: 01223-353552 (Ground)
01223-336789 (Hon. Treasurer)   Fax: 01223-331157
0966-225278 (Club Administrator)

Description of ground:
The University Club's home since 1848. Also had an athletics track until the 1950s. There is a new pavilion, but very little other development. Very pleasant university setting in classical Cambridge. Modern flats overlook one corner. Very limited facilities for spectators, but bring a deck chair and watch the cricket on a sunny day. Some bench seating available. Ground admission is free except for British Universities matches involving touring teams.

Catering and bars:
Bar and limited food in pavilion. For major matches, beer tent, sandwiches, fast food available. Otherwise shops on Mill Road.

Shops:
No club shop. Newsletter available at bar in pavilion

General facilities:
Cricket coaching facilities: No
Cricket nets: No
Other sporting or recreational facilities on the ground: No
Facilities for hire or wider community use at the ground: Yes. Pavilion can be hired for functions, and ground for matches.
Ticket office: None
Scoreboards: One, square of wicket.
Toilets: By entrance and in pavilion.

Entrance: On Mortimer Road.

Facilities and access for people with disabilities:
Wheelchair access to the ground: Yes.
Designated car parking available inside the ground: No.
Viewing areas for people using wheelchairs: Yes. No designated areas but plenty of flat ground.
Ramps to provide easy access to bars and refreshment outlets: No.
No toilets for people with disabilities.

Travel:
Car parking: Free for members. Multi-storey car park by ground. Street parking very restricted
Nearest station: Cambridge
Buses: Any for city centre or going to Hills Road.
Tourist information: Cambridge TIC, Wheeler St, CB2 3QB.
Tel: 01223-322640. Fax: 01223-457588.

Road directions:
Ground is in city centre, by traffic lights where Gonville Place (A603) meets Mill Road. A603 from M11 junction 12 or A1134 from M11 junction 11 lead to Gonville Road.

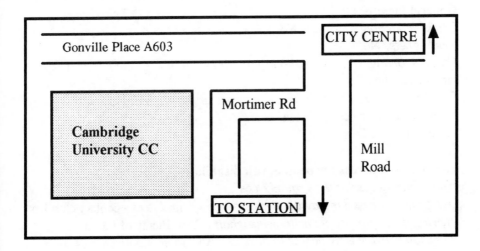

Oxford University CC
The Parks

Ground address: The Parks, Parks Road, Oxford, Oxfordshire
Club address: Dr S. R. Porter, Oxford University CC, University Parks, Oxford OX1 3RF
Telephone: 01865-557106.   **Fax:** 01865-557106.
Capacity: Up to 10,000.

Description of ground:
Very attractive setting in a University park. Home of Oxford University cricket - first used in 1881. Outside the city centre, the park also stages other University sports. Limited spectator facilities, but a pleasant venue for watching the students challenge the county professionals. Some benches provided or bring a deck chair.

Catering and bars:
Bar and snacks available.

Shops:
No club shop.

General facilities:
Cricket coaching facilities: No.
Cricket nets: No
Other sporting or recreational facilities on the ground: Other sports facilities in the park.
Facilities for hire or wider community use at the ground: No.
Scoreboard: One near pavilion.
Toilets: By pavilion.

Facilities and access for people with disabilities:
Wheelchair access to the ground: Yes.
Designated car parking available inside the ground: Yes - contact club first
Viewing areas for people using wheelchairs: Yes. Plenty of flat areas.
Ramps to provide easy access to bars and refreshment outlets: Yes.

Travel:
Car parking: Local car parks (not very close). Street parking very restricted.
Nearest station: Oxford.
Buses: City circuit electric bus, no.5. 7, 7a, 10, 25, 25a, 27, all stop at Wycliffe Hall.. Information: 01865-772250.
Tourist information: Oxford TIC, The Old School, Gloucester Green, OX1 2DA. Tel: 01865-726871. Fax: 01865-240261.

Road directions:
The Parks is north of the city centre. Take the A40 (Northern by pass), and at Cutteslowe roundabout with the A4165, turn south (signposted Summertown) into Banbury Road. Turn left into Parks Road by School of Engineering, and University Parks is on left. The ground is in the park.

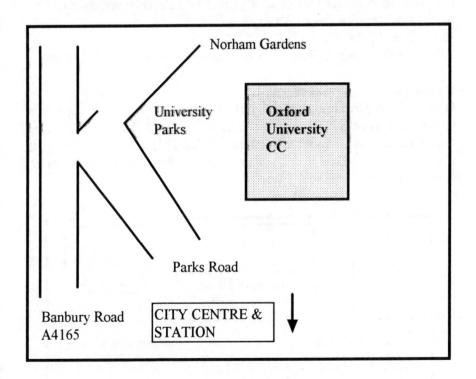

Scotland

Edinburgh: Grange Cricket Club,
Address: The Pavilion, Raeburn Place, Edinburgh EH4 1HQ
Telephone: 0131-332-2148

Description of ground:
Attractive club ground near the centre of Edinburgh. Impressive pavilion and some permanent seating, supplemented by temporary seating for major matches. Also has facilities for hockey, tennis and squash. The venue for two Scotland 1999 World Cup matches

Travel
Car parking: None for the public at ground. Some in surrounding streets.
Nearest station: Edinburgh Waverley
Buses: 19a, 20, 28, 80.
Tourist information: 3, Princes Street, Edinburgh EH2. 0131-557-1700

Road directions
Ground is in Stockbridge, on the B900. From Princes St go west into Queensferry Street which leads into Queensferry Road. Turn right into Dean Park Crescent and immediately left into Comely Bank Avenue. Turn right into Comely Bank Road which becomes Raeburn Place and ground is on left, with entrance in Port Gower Place.

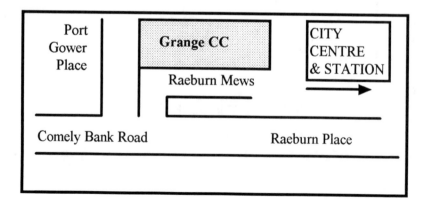

Scottish Cricket Union
R.W. Barclay (Hon. Secretary)
Caledonia House, South Gyle, Edinburgh EH12 9DQ
Telephone: 0131-317-7247   **Fax:** 0131-317-7103

Other Scotland grounds:

Glasgow Titwood
Teacher's Clydesdale Cricket Club, The Pavilion, Titwood Athletic Grounds,
Beaton Road, Pollokshields, Glasgow G41 4LA
Telephone: 0141-423-1463

Forfar
Strathmore Cricket Club, The Pavilion, Lochside Park, Forfar
Telephone: 01307-464289

Ireland

Clontarf
Address: Clontarf Cricket Club, Castle Avenue, Dublin
Telephone: (353)-01-833-2621

Ground is north east of city centre. The venue for the West Indies versus Bangladesh match in the 1999 World Cup.

Travel
Nearest station: Clontarf Road or Killester. From Clontarf Road station walk east down Clontarf Road to Castle Avenue. Killester station is near junction of Howth Road with Castle Avenue.
Information: (353)-01-836-6222
Buses: 31, 31a, 31b, 32, 32a, 32b all run up Howth Road. Get off at Castle Grove, walk through to Castle Avenue. 103 runs down Castle Avenue.
Tourist information: Dublin Tourist Information, 14, Upper O'Connell Street. (353)-01-284-4768.
Irish Tourist Board: 150, New Bond Street, London W1. 0171-493-3201.

Road directions
Take Howth Road towards Killester. Turn right into Castle Avenue and ground is on right. Alternatively, take Clontarf Road towards Clontarf, turn left into Castle Avenue and ground is on left.

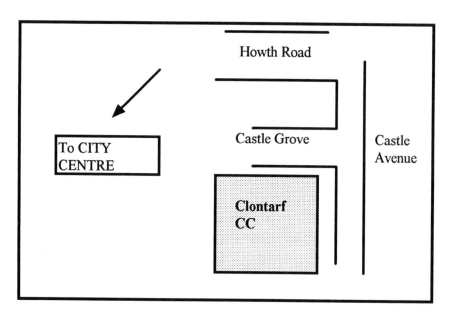

Irish Cricket Union
D. Scott (Hon Secretary)
45, Foxcroft Park, Dublin 18
Telephone: (353)-01-289-3943 Fax: (353)-01-845-5545

Other Ireland grounds:

Malahide
Malahide Cricket Club, Malahide, County Dublin, Ireland
Telephone: (353)-01-845-0607

Downpatrick
Downpatrick Cricket Club, Strangford Road, Downpatrick, N.Ireland
Telephone: 01396-612869

The Netherlands

Koninklijke Nederlandse Cricket Bond
Nieuwe Kalfjeslaan 21B, 1182AA Amstelveen, The Netherlands
Telephone: (31)-020-645-1705   Fax: (31)-020-645-1715

Amstelveen
VRA Cricket Ground
Address: Nieuwe Kalfjeslaan 21B, 1182AA Amstelveen, The Netherlands
Telephone: (31)-020-641-8525 or (31)-020-645-9816
Fax: (31)-020-643-4616

About the ground
The VRA Ground in Amstelveen (near Amsterdam) was the second Dutch
ground to install a grass wicket. The 5-strip square has been used for many
VRA home matches, several practice matches for Dutch elevens, and has
staged international matches. The South African touring party played the
Dutch national team here in July 1998. The first 3-day match was played in
August 1998, when India 'A' visited The Netherlands for a series of
matches. The ground is the venue for the 1999 World Cup match between
South Africa and Kenya. The offices of the Royal Dutch Cricket Association
are located in the pavilion

Travel
Tourist information: Netherlands Board of Tourism, PO Box 523, London
SW1. Telephone: 0891-717777 (premium rates).
Car parking: Parking available at ground.
Nearest station: Buses from Amsterdam Central, Amstel or South/World
Trade Centre.
Buses:
From Amsterdam Central Train Station : Numbers 170, 171, 172.
From Amstel Train Station : Number 169.
From Train Station South/World Trade Centre: Number 63.
From RAI Train Station : Number 169.
From Haarlemmermeer Buss station: Numbers 147, 170, 171, 172.

For all buses: Get off at "Kalfjeslaan (in Amstelveen - a suburb of Amsterdam). Go into "Nieuwe Kalfjeslaan - opposite church into Amsterdamse Bos (Forest).
Over railway, straight on for approximately 1,500 metres. Follow road signs VRA/ACC/Pinoke until you come to the parking area. Club house can be seen on the left-hand-side.
Just before the parking area turn left. VRA Cricket Ground is 200 metres on the left.

Road directions
From Utrecht: Follow signs on highway Amstelveen. Take exit -Amstelveen Centre. Turn right at the traffic lights.
Follow this road (beginning is called Keizer Karelweg and continues as Amsterdamse Weg for 2,000 metres).
Turn left opposite Church into Nieuwe Kalfjeslaan. Pass over railway, straight on for approximately 1,500 metres. Follow road signs VRA/ACC/Pinoke until parking area. Club house can be seen on the left hand-side. Just before parking area turn left. VRA Cricket Ground is 200 metres on the left

From The Hague, Rotterdam, and Haarlem : Follow signs-Amstelveen on highway.
Take exit Amstelveen Centre, turn right at traffic lights, under highway, follow this road (beginning is called Keizer Karelweg and continues as Amsterdamse Weg for 2,000 metres). Continue as above.

We would like to thank the Koninklijke Nederlandse Cricket Bond for providing the above information.

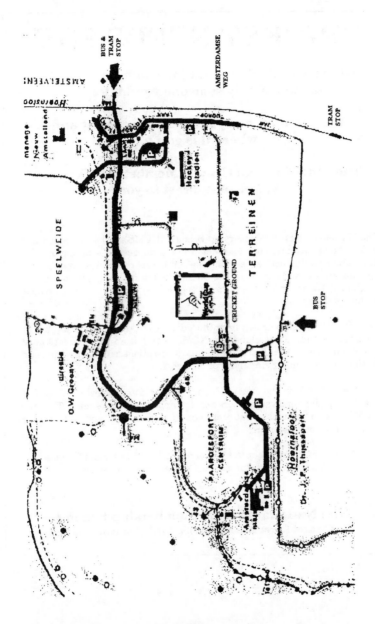

Map provided by Koninklijke Nederlandse Cricket Bond

107

CRICKET NEEDS YOU

Feel you could add something useful to cricketing debates if only someone would listen?

Want to have a say in who runs cricket and where it is going?

Then the National Cricket Membership Scheme will be of interest to you.

The National Cricket Membership Scheme (NCMS) seeks to deepen and widen the participation of cricket-followers in the decision-making process. This it has done by actively seeking the opinions of the cricketing public via opinion surveys and supplying the findings to cricket's administration. The England & Wales Cricket Board has acknowledged the value, and taken note, of these surveys.

With its membership drawn from the 'general' cricketing public as well as members of the county clubs, the NCMS is free from the accusations of parochialism that are often made against propositions or opinions expressed by the counties, either singularly or en masse.

English cricket is in the midst of an age of reform and we believe it is vital that the opinions of its supporters are researched and represented. Thus the NCMS has no 'manifesto' but seeks simply to be a focus and voice for the views of cricket supporters.

To find out more about the National Cricket Membership Scheme please forward a stamped and self-addressed envelope to:

The National Cricket Membership Scheme
C/o Cricket Lore 22 Grazebrook Road London N16 0HS

Outgrounds

This section includes all current outgrounds used by first class counties, Shenley Cricket Centre and Oakham School which are staging tourist matches in 1999.

Durham CCC

Darlington Cricket Club

Address: Feethams Cricket Ground, South Terrace, Darlington, DL1 5JD
Telephone: 01325-466415
Capacity: 5,000

Travel:
Car parking: Very limited at ground. Street parking and town centre car parks
Nearest station: Darlington
Buses: Depot very near ground. X27 and X28. Information: 0345-124125.
Tourist information: Darlington TIC, 13, Horsemarket, DL1 5PW. 01325-388666. Fax: 01325-388667

Road directions:
From A66, take A167 (Grange Rd) towards town centre. Turn right onto Victoria Rd (still A167- dual carriageway), and ground is on right, next to supermarket. Turn round at next roundabout for access.

Hartlepool Cricket Club

Address: The Pavilion, Park Drive, West Park, Hartlepool, TS26 0DA
Telephone: 012429-260875
Capacity: 3,500
Travel:

Car parking: Very limited at ground. Street parking and at local schools.
Nearest station: Hartlepool
Buses: Information: 01429-523555
Tourist information: Hartlepool TIC, Hartlepool Art Gallery, Church Sq., TS24 7EQ.
01429-869706. Fax:01429-523408

Road directions:
From A689 (Stockton St), turn left into Park Rd. Turn right at T junction into Elwick Rd, and immediately left (still Elwick Rd). Pass Ward Jackson Park on right, turn right (still Elwick Rd) and ground is on left.

Stockton Cricket Club

Address: The Grangefield Road Ground, Oxbridge Avenue, Stockton-on-Tees, TS18 4JF
Telephone: 01642-672835
Capacity: 4,000

Travel:
Car parking: Members & general public. Additional parking provided - very limited at ground.
Nearest station: Stockton
Buses: Information: 01642-444777

Tourist information: Stockton on Tees TIC, Theatre Yard, Off High St, TS18 1AT. 01642-393936. Fax:01642-616315.

Road directions:
From town centre: A135 towards Yarm. Fork right into Oxbridge Lane (signposted local). Next roundabout turn right (signposted Norton A1027) into Oxbridge Avenue. Ground on right, opposite Grangefield School. From A66, take A135 (Yarm Rd) towards town centre, turn left into Oxbridge Lane, then as above.

Essex CCC

Colchester & East Essex CC

Address: Castle Park (Lower), Sports Way, Colchester, Essex
Telephone: 01206-574028
Capacity: 6,000

Travel:
Car parking: Large car park in ground, members free, public £2.
Nearest station: Colchester St. Botolph's or Colchester North.
Buses: Bus station off High Street, 0.75 miles from ground. Information: Eastern National: 01206-571451, Colchester Borough Transport: 01206-764029
Tourist information: Colchester TIC, 1, Queen St, CO1 2PJ. 01206-282920.Fax: 01206-282924.

Road directions:
Take A133 from A12. This becomes Colne Bank Avenue. Go straight over roundabout with A134. Follow signs for Leisure World, but before reaching there, take next right into Catchpool Road. This leads into Sports Way, by ground.

Ilford Cricket Club

Address: Valentine's Park, Cranbrook Road, Ilford, Essex
Telephone: 0181-554-8381
Capacity: 5,000

Travel:
Car parking: None at ground. Field in park for members & public.
Nearest station: Ilford (train) or Gants Hill (underground)
Buses: 123, 179, & 396.
Information: 0171-222-1234
Tourist information:
Redbridge TIC, Town Hall, High Rd, IG1 1DD. 0181-478-3020. Fax: 0181-478-9149

Road directions:
A12 Gants Hill roundabout (i.e. with A1400 and A123): take A123 (Cranbrook Road) south from roundabout - signposted Ilford & Barking. Ground is on left hand side, around 0.5 miles from roundabout.

Southend-on-Sea CC

Address: Southchurch Park,
Northumberland Crescent,
Southend on Sea
Telephone: 01702-615195 (County
matches only)
Capacity: 6,000

Travel:
Car parking: Some at ground -free
for members. Otherwise Lifstan Road
car park.
Nearest station: Southend East
Buses: Eastern National 20,
Shoeburyness to Hullbridge passes
train stations Southend Central and
Victoria. 7, 7a, 7c & 8.
Information: Southend Public
Transport:01702-434444
Thamesway: 01245-262828
Tourist information: Southend-on-
Sea TIC, 19, High St, SS2 1JE.
01702-215120.
Fax: 01702-431449.

Road directions:
Ground is to the east of town centre.
Take A13 (Southchurch Rd) from
town centre, turn right onto Lifstan
Way, and ground is on right.
Alternative: drive along sea front -
Eastern Esplanade (B1016) and turn
left into Lifstan Way.

Glamorgan CCC

Abergavenny Cricket Club

Address: Pen-y-Pound Cricket
Ground, Avenue Road, Abergavenny,
Gwent
Telephone: 01873-852350
Capacity: 5,000

Travel:
Car parking: Limited at ground.
Additional parking at football
ground, and street parking.
Nearest station: Abergavenny
Buses: Bus station 1.5 miles from
ground, by Tourist Information
Office. Shuttle service from bus
station for matches.
Information: 01633-266336
Tourist information:
Abergavenny TIC, Swan Meadow,
Monmouth Rd, NP7 5HH.
01873-857588

Road directions:
From roundabout of A40 with
Merthyr Road by pass and Mount
Street, go towards town centre. Turn
left into Chapel Road, right into
Harold Road which leads into
Avenue Road. For parking, turn left
into Pen-y-Pound for football
ground. Access also from Old
Hereford Rd. From Heads of the
Valleys Road, (A465), take A4143
Merthyr Road towards town centre,
at roundabout take first turning into
Merthyr Road by pass, right at
roundabout, then as above.

Colwyn Bay Cricket Club

Address: Penrhyn Avenue, Rhos-on-Sea, Colwyn Bay, Clwyd LL28 4LR
Telephone: 01492-544103 or 545082
Capacity: 4,750 with temporary seating

Travel:
Car parking: Limited at ground. Additional parking provided, and street parking.
Nearest station: Colwyn Bay. Information: 0345-484950
Buses: 12,14 or any towards Llandudno. Stop by ground. Information: 01492-596969.
Tourist information: Colwyn Bay Imperial Buildings, Station Square, Princes Drive, LL29 8LF TIC, 01492-530478.
Fax: 01492-534789

Road directions:
Ground is in Rhos-on-Sea, rather than Colwyn Bay. From Colwyn Bay town centre, take promenade north towards Rhos-on-Sea. Turn left into Penrhyn Avenue. From A55, take turning signposted Rhos on Sea, follow signs for Rhos-on-Sea. At roundabout, turn into Brompton Avenue, right at traffic lights into Rhos Road, left into Colwyn Crescent, and left into Penrhyn Avenue.

Pontypridd Cricket Club

Address: Pontypridd CC, The Pavilion, Ynysangharad Park, Pontypridd
Telephone: 01443-404699 (park) or 490155 (Cricket Club clubhouse)
Capacity: 5,000 (with temporary seating)

Travel:
Car parking: Very limited at ground. Some street parking and local car parks.
Nearest station: Pontypridd.
Buses: Bus station in town centre C18, C19, 120, 130.
Information:
Rhondda: 01443-682671
Caerphilly: 01222-867003
Shamrock: 01443-407000
Tourist information: Bridge St, CF37 3PE
01443-409512. Fax: 01443-485565

Road directions:
A470 take turning for Pontypridd inner relief road, signposted Pontypridd. Use local car parks, and ground is across bridge from Taff Street.

Swansea Cricket & Football Club

Address: Swansea Cricket and Football Club, St Helen's Cricket Ground, Bryn Road, Swansea, West Glamorgan SA2 0AR
Telephone: 01792-424242
Capacity: 3,750 plus temporary seating

Travel:
Car parking: None at ground.
Local car parks, and street parking.
Nearest station: Swansea 1.5 miles
Buses: 16, 37, to King Edward Road
Information: 01792-580580
Tourist information: Swansea Tourist
Information Centre, Singleton St,
Swansea SA1 3QG. 01792-468321

Road directions: From city centre
take Oystermouth Road along coast
(A4067), heading west. Pass County
Hall on left. This road becomes
Mumbles Road. Ground on right. No
AA signs but aim for the Mumbles.
Limited parking opposite, but much
more a bit further on.

Gloucestershire CCC

Cheltenham College

Address: College Sports Ground,
Cheltenham College, Thirlestaine
Road, Cheltenham
Telephone: 01242-522000
Capacity: 4,000
Travel:
Car parking: In ground or at
overflow (400 yards away).
Nearest station: Cheltenham Spa
(1 mile)
Buses: Q to hospital.
Information: 01452-526 662
Tourist information: Cheltenham
TIC, 77, Promenade, GL50 1PP.
01242-522878. Fax: 01242-255848

Road directions: The ground is
situated south of the town centre.

Thirlestaine Road is off the A46
(Bath Road). Well signed routes
from the M5 and good on ground
parking with overspill nearby for late
arrivals.

King's School, Gloucester

Address: Archdeacon Meadow,
King's School, St Oswald's Road,
Gloucester
Telephone: 01452-423011
Capacity: 2,500

Travel:
Car parking: At ground
Nearest station: Gloucester Central
Buses: Information: 01703-529090.
Park & ride on Saturdays.
Tourist information: Gloucester TIC,
28 Southgate St, GL1 2PD. 01452-
421188. Fax: 01452-504273.

Road directions:
Ground on A417 (St Oswald's Road),
just south of junction with A40. To
north of city centre. 0.25 miles from
Cathedral. From M5 junction 12,
A38 then A430 towards city centre.
From M5 junction 11, A40 then
A417.

Hampshire CCC

Basingstoke & North Hants CC

Address: May's Bounty, Bounty
Road, Basingstoke, Hampshire,
RG21 2DR.
Telephone: 01256-473646
Capacity: 3,000

113

Travel:
Car parking: Adjacent to ground.
Street parking very restricted.
Nearest station: Basingstoke
Buses: 39 to Winchester Rd, 40 to
Hackwood Rd from town bus centre.
Information: 01256-464501
Tourist information: Basingstoke
TIC, Willis Museum, Old Town Hall,
Market Place, RG21 7QD.
01256-817618. Fax: 01256-356231.

Road directions:
M3 Junction 6. Turn left at
roundabout onto ring road, and at
next roundabout turn right into
Hackwood Rd. Turn left into
Southern Road, cross Victoria Street
into Bounty Road - ground on left.

Portsmouth - United Services CC

Address: Burnaby Road,
Portsmouth, Hampshire, PO1 2EJ
Telephone: 01705-830125
Capacity: 4,500

Travel:
Road restrictions on match days: No
parking in Burnaby Rd.
Car parking: Opposite ground
entrance. Some street parking a few
minutes walk from ground. Also
local car parks.
Nearest station: Portsmouth &
Southsea.
Buses: Information: 01705-862412
Tourist information:
Portsmouth TIC, The Hard,
Portsmouth PO1 3QJ.
01705-826722.Fax: 01705-822693.

Road directions:
M275 into city centre, then A3 follow
signs for Portsea or ferries. AA signs
for county cricket. Burnaby Road is
right turn off Cambridge Road.

Kent CCC

Maidstone - The Mote CC

Address: Mote Park, Willow Way,
Maidstone, Kent.
Telephone: 01622-754159.
For Kent matches: 01622-754545
Capacity: 8,000

Travel:
Car parking: Some at ground. Street
parking very restricted.
Nearest station: Maidstone East or
Maidstone West
Buses: Near bus station. 85 from
High Street and Chequers Centre.
Kent Council transport
information: 0345-696996
Tourist information: Maidstone TIC,
The Gatehouse, Palace Gardens, Mill
Street, ME16 6YE. 01622-602169.
Fax: 01622-673581.

Road directions:
From town centre, take A20 (Ashford
Rd). Turn right into Square Hill, and
continue into Square Hill Road. At
roundabout, turn left into Mote
Avenue, and follow road round into
Willow Way. Ground on left.

Tunbridge Wells Cricket Club

Address: Nevill Cricket Ground, Nevill Gate, Warwick Park, TN2 5ES
Telephone: 01892-520846
Capacity: 5,500

Travel:
Road restrictions on match days: No parking in roads near ground.
Car parking: Some at ground. Park and ride scheme.
Nearest station: Tunbridge Wells
Buses: Stop on Forest Rd.
Kent Council transport information: 0345-696996
Special transport arrangements on match days: Park and ride. Signposted.
Tourist information:
Tunbridge Wells TIC, The Old Fish Market, The Pantiles, TN2 5TN. 01892-515675. Fax: 01892-534660

Road directions:
From A21 take A264 (Pembury Rd) towards town centre. Turn left into Kingswood Rd, and then left into Bayhall Rd. Follow road round. This becomes Forest Road. Warwick Park is on right, and ground is after playing field on right hand side.

Lancashire CCC

Blackpool Cricket Club

Address: Stanley Park, West Park Drive, Blackpool, Lancashire, FY3 9GQ
Telephone: 01253-393347

Capacity: 8,000

Travel:
Car parking: Some adjoining ground. Also in Stanley Park. Some street parking.
Nearest station: Blackpool North
Buses: 21,44b from Talbot Rd to Stanley Park gates. Information: 01253-473000
Tourist information:
Blackpool TIC, 1, Clifton St, FY1 1LY. 01253-478222.
Fax: 01253-478213

Road directions:
M55 take Junction 4. Take left hand lane for North Shore. Turn right into South Park Drive. At mini roundabout, turn left into West Park Drive. Drive along park, past sports centre. Ground on right.

Liverpool Cricket Club

Address: The Pavilion, Aigburth Road, Grassendale, Liverpool, L19 3QF
Telephone: 0151-427-2930.
Capacity: 8,000 (county matches)

Travel:
Road restrictions on match days: No parking near ground.
Car parking: On lower ground at end of Riversdale Rd. Also street parking.
Nearest station: Aigburth or Cressington. 0151-236-7676
Buses: 20, 26, 32, 82.
Information: 0151-236-7676

Tourist information: Merseyside Welcome Centre, Clayton Sq. Shopping Centre, L1 1QR. 0151-709-3631. Fax: 0151-708-0204

Road directions:
On A561 Aigburth Rd south of city centre, leading to Widnes and Runcorn. At junction with Riversdale Rd. Ground is signposted.

Lytham Cricket Club

Address: Church Road, Lytham, FY8 5DQ
Telephone: 01253-734137
Capacity: 5,000

Travel:
Car parking: At ground. Street parking available. Also YMCA ground 400 yards away.
Nearest station: Lytham
Buses: 11,11a, 193. Information: 01253-473000.
Tourist information: Lytham St Anne's TIC, 290, Clifton Drive South, FY8 1LH. 01253-725610. Fax: 01253-713754

Road directions:
M55 take junction 4. Take A5230 towards South Shore. Turn left at traffic lights into Common Edge Road B5261, signposted Lytham St Anne's. Stay on this road, which becomes Church Road, and ground on left.
Alternative: Take A584 along sea front, turn left into Woodville Terrace, and ground at end of road.

Southport & Birkdale CC

Address: The Pavilion, Trafalgar Rd, Birkdale, Southport, PR8 2HF
Telephone: 01704-569951
Capacity: 5,000

Travel:
Car parking: None at ground. Street parking restricted. Use Royal Birkdale Golf Club.
Nearest station: Southport. Local service: Birkdale or Hillside
Buses: 5 from town centre. Stop on Grosvenor Rd.
Information: 0151-236-7676
Tourist information: Southport TIC, 112 Lord St PR8 1NY. 01704-533333

Road directions:
Take A565 south from town centre. Turn left into Grosvenor Road, and right into Trafalgar Rd, and ground is on left. Coming from south, use A565, turn right into Grosvenor Rd, then as above. Parking at Royal Birkdale Golf Club.

Middlesex CCC

Southgate Cricket Club

Address: Waterfall Road, London N14 7JZ
Telephone: 0181-886-8381
Capacity: 3,000

Travel:
Car parking: Some at ground, also street parking.

Nearest station: Southgate (London Underground), New Southgate (train) *Bus:* 121, 299, W6. Information: 0171-222-1234. *Tourist information:* 0839-123456 (Premium rate).

Road directions:
From M25, take A111 south to Southgate Circus roundabout. Turn right onto High Street (A1004), and then right into Waterfall Road (A1003). From North Circular (A406), take Green Lane (A105) north , turn left into Alderman's Hill (A1004), follow road to right - becomes Cannon Hill and turn left into Waterfall Road (A1003).

Uxbridge Cricket Club

Address: Gatting Way, Park Road, Uxbridge
Telephone: 01895-237571
Capacity: 3,500

Travel:
Car parking: At ground.
Nearest station: Uxbridge (London Underground)
Information: 0171-222-1234
Buses: U1, U2, U10. Bus station by underground station.
Information: 0171-222-1234

Special transport arrangements on match days: Occasionally provided.
Tourist Information:
Hillingdon TIC, Central Library, 14-15 High St, Uxbridge UB81 1HD.
Tel: 01895-250706

Fax: 01895-239794

Road directions:
From A40, take B483(Park Road) south towards Uxbridge, and ground is on left. This A40 junction is the last one before the start of the M40, leaving London. AA signs used when Middlesex playing at Uxbridge.

Northamptonshire CCC

Luton Town CC

Address: Wardown Park, Old Bedford Road, Luton, Bedfordshire
Telephone: 01582-27855
Capacity: 5,000

Travel:
Car parking: In Wardown Park
Nearest station: Luton
Buses: 24 (by library), 25, 26 - stop on Old Bedford Road. Information: 0345-788788. Green Line 757.
Tourist information: Luton TIC, The Bus Station, Bute Street, LU1 2EY. 01582-401579.
Fax: 01582-487886

Road directions:
From M1 junction 11 take A505 towards town centre. Pass first sign for Bedford A6, but after entering one way system, follow signs for Bedford A6. At roundabout by park, turn right, and right again at traffic lights into Old Bedford Road.

117

Milton Keynes - Campbell Park

Address: Campbell Park, Silbury Boulevard, Milton Keynes
Telephone: 01908-694820
Capacity: 5,000 approx.

Travel:
Car parking: Limited at ground. In park and some street parking.
Nearest station: Milton Keynes Central
Buses: 1, 17 (from station), 1E, 90, 19E all stop near ground.
Information: 0345-382000.
Tourist information: Milton Keynes TIC, 411, Secklow Gate East, The Food Hall, MK9 3NE. 01908-232525.
Fax: 01908-235050.

Road directions:
From M1 junction 14, take A509 (H5 Portway) towards city centre. Turn left at roundabout into North Overgate, and ground is straight ahead, over Cricket Green Roundabout. Campbell Park is well signposted.

Nottinghamshire CCC

Cleethorpes CC
Address: Chichester Road, Cleethorpes, DN35.
Telephone: 01472-691271

Travel:
Car parking: Two car parks nearby
Nearest station: Cleethorpes

Buses: 8 from High Street to sea front.
Tourist information: 42-43 Alexandra Road, Cleethorpes, Humberside, DN35 8LE 01472-323111. Fax: 01472-323112.

Road directions: A46 towards Cleethorpes. At roundabout turn right onto Humberston Road (A1031). At next roundabout turn left into Taylors Avenue. Turn right into Chichester Road (after King George V Playing Field) and ground is on left.

Worksop Town CC

Address: Central Avenue, Worksop, Nottinghamshire
Telephone: 01909-472681
Capacity: 7,000

Travel:
Car parking: At ground. Members free, public pay. Also local car parks and street parking.
Nearest station: Worksop
Buses: Bus station very close to ground.
Information: 01777-710550
Tourist information: Worksop TIC, Worksop Library, Memorial Avenue S80 2BP. 01909- 501148. Fax: 01909-501148.

Road directions:
Ground is very close to roundabout where A57 meets A60. From this roundabout take A60 Newcastle Avenue into town centre. Turn left

118

into Stubbing Lane, and immediately right into Central Avenue. Entrance to ground is 0.25 miles along, opposite Allen Street.

Somerset CCC

Bath Recreation Ground

Address: The Pavilion, The Recreation Ground, William St, Bath
Telephone: 01225-424970
Capacity: 6,000

Travel:
Car parking: At ground: members and public. Also local car parks, and park and ride (except Saturday)
Nearest station: Bath Spa
Buses: Information: 01225-464446
Tourist information: Bath TIC, Abbey Chambers, Abbey Church Yard, BA1 1LY. 01225-477101. Fax: 01225-477787.

Road directions:
Ground is off A36 (Pulteney Road) to east of city centre. Turn into Edward St at roundabout, and then left into Pulteney Mews. If coming along Great Pulteney Street, turn into William Street, and then into Pulteney Mews. Entrance from city centre from Argyle Street via Pulteney Bridge and right after the shops and do not confuse with Bath Cricket Club ground on the other side of North Parade.

Surrey CCC

Guildford Cricket Club

Address: Woodbridge Road, Guildford, Surrey, GU1
Telephone: 01483-572181
Capacity: 3,500

Travel:
Car parking: Limited at ground. Some at Guildford Technical College - Stoke Rd. Also local car parks. Very limited street parking.
Nearest station: Guildford
Buses: Information: 01483-575226. 5,16,20 and 28 from bus station by Friary Centre.
Tourist information: Guildford TIC, 14, Tunsgate, GU1 3QT. 01483-444333.
Fax: 01483: 302046.

Road directions:
From A3 south, take A3100 turn off into Guildford. At roundabout, go west on A25. Go straight over roundabout with A320, and take next left at traffic lights, Woodbridge Road. Ground on right hand side. From A3 north, turn off onto A25. Go east and turn right into Woodbridge Road. Ground on right hand side.

Sussex CCC

Friends of Arundel Castle CC
Address: Arundel Park, Arundel, E. Sussex, BN18 9LH
Telephone: 01903-882462

Capacity: 9,000

Travel:
Car parking: In ground. Do not park by the Castle entrance - it's a long walk.
Nearest station: Arundel
Buses: 702 from station.
Information: 01903-237661
Tourist information: Arundel TIC, 61, High St BN18 9AJ.
01903-882268.
Fax: 01903-882419

Road directions:
From A27, turn north at roundabout with A284 (direction Petworth), then first right into London Road and entrance to ground is on left.
From A29, take A284 into Arundel, turn left into London Road, and entrance to ground is on left.

Eastbourne Saffrons Sports Club

Address: Eastbourne Saffrons Sports Club, The Saffrons, Compton Place Road, Eastbourne, E. Sussex, BN21 1EA
Telephone: 01323-724328
Capacity: 4,500

Travel:
Car parking: Inside ground.
Nearest station: Eastbourne
Buses: Information: 01323-416416. Any bus to Terminus Road.
Tourist information: Eastbourne TIC, Cornfield Rd, BN21 4QL. 01323-411400.
Fax: 01323-649574.

Road directions:
From A27 and A22: Come into Eastbourne on A22 (Willingdon Rd). This becomes Upperton Rd. At roundabout, turn right into Grove Road. Turn right at end of road, and right again into Saffrons Road. The ground is very close to the town hall and the courts.

Horsham Cricket Club
Address: Cricketfield Road, Worthing Road, Horsham, W. Sussex, RH12 1TE
Telephone: 01403-254628
Capacity: 4,500
Travel:
Car parking: In ground.
Nearest station: Horsham
Buses: Information: 0345-959099. 2,55 and 97 from station. 65,70 and 86 from bus station off Albion Way.
Tourist information: Horsham TIC, 9, Causeway, RH12 1HE. 01403-211661.

Road directions:
From A24 Horsham by pass, take A281 towards town centre. Turn right into Blackbridge Lane. At end of road, turn left into Worthing Road, and then immediately right into Cricketfield Road. Ground on right.

Worcestershire CCC

Kidderminster Cricket Club

Address: Chester Road Sports Club, Offmore Lane, Chester Rd, Kidderminster, DY10 1TH

Telephone: 01562-824175
Capacity: 3,000 - can be expanded

Travel:
Car parking: In ground for members and public. Also local street parking.
Nearest station: Kidderminster (0.5 miles)
Buses: Hopper buses from town centre.
Tourist information: Kidderminster TIC, Severn Valley Railway Station, Comberton Hill, DY10 1QX. 01562-829400. (1 May to September) or 01299-404740.

Road directions:
No yellow AA signs. From M5 junction 3, A456 towards town centre, turn left into Chester Road, and Ground on left. Ground is just to east of town centre, by Comberton estate.

Yorkshire CCC

Scarborough Cricket Club

Address: North Marine Road, Scarborough, YO12 7TJ
Telephone: 01723-365625.
Fax: 01273-364287.
Capacity: 15,000

Travel:
Car parking: None at ground. Local car parks and limited street parking.
Nearest station: Scarborough.
Buses: Bus station in town centre. 01723-375463.

Tourist information: Scarborough TIC, Unit 3, Pavilion House, Valley Bridge Rd, YO11 1UZ. 01723-373333. Fax: 01723-363785.

Road directions:
From town centre, take Victoria Road towards North Sands and North Bay. This becomes Castle Road, and at roundabout, take North Marine Road on the left. Ground on left 300 yards further on.

Other grounds

The Denis Compton Ground Shenley Cricket Centre

Address: Radlett Lane, Shenley, Hertfordshire WD7 9DW
Telephone: 01923-859022

Travel:
Car parking: Not at ground. Car Park in Shenley Park.
Nearest station: Radlett (then bus or taxi), or Watford Junction (then bus or taxi).
Buses: 602 or B9 stop by ground. Information 0345-244344. Sovereign buses at end of Radlett Lane. Information 01707-376582.
Tourist information: St Albans TIC, Town Hall, Market Place, St Albans, Herts AL3 5DJ

Road directions:
From South: From A1 take A5135 signposted Boreham Wood. Fork right to Shenley and Well End. Go

The Hertfordshire Cricket Society

The Pavilion, The Denis Compton Ground, Shenley Cricket Centre,
Shenley Park, Radlett Lane, Shenley, Herts WD7 9DW
Telephone / fax: 01923-859022

Main objectives:

- Monthly meetings during autumn/winter period with guest speakers
- To provide a forum for members to meet and hear speakers
- To produce a yearbook, newsletter and tie
- To promote the interest and preservation of the Denis Compton Ground
- To establish a Society playing XI

Annual subscription is £10.00

For further information please contact W.A. Powell, Hon. Secretary at the address above.

through Well End and in Shenley turn left at second roundabout. Then turn immediately left into Radlett Lane (signposted Shenley Park). Entrance to ground is signposted on right.
From north: J22 on M25. Take B556 west towards Radlett and turn left onto B5378. This goes into the centre of Shenley. Turn right at roundabout signposted Shenley Park and then as above.

Oakham School

Address: Doncaster Close, Kilburn Road, Oakham, Rutland LE15 6Ql
Telephone: 01572-758582

Travel:
Nearest station: Oakham
(2 minutes walk)

Road directions:
From south A1, A606 to Oakham
From North: A1, take B668 to Oakham
From West: A14 to Kettering / Corby / Stamford, take A6003 to Oakham. Ground is behind the Police Station

(Our thanks to Oakham School for providing the above information).

Minor Counties Grounds

(Our thanks to Mike Berry for his assistance with this section).

Minor Counties Cricket Association:
Secretary: Mr D.J.M. Armstrong
Thorpe Cottage, Mill Common,
Ridlington, North Walsham
NR28 9TY.
Tel/fax: 01692-650563

Bedfordshire CCC

Bedford Town CC
Goldington Bury,
Church Lane,
Goldington, Bedford
Tel: 01234-352458

Dunstable Town CC
Lancot Park,
Dunstable Road,
Totternhoe,
Dunstable
Tel: 01582-663735

Henlow CC
Henlow Park,
Groveside,
Henlow
Tel: 01462-811218

Luton Town CC
Wardown Park,
Old Bedford Road, Luton
Tel: 01582-27855
(see page 117)

Southill Park CC
Southill Park Estate,
Southill
Tel: None

Berkshire CCC

Falkland CC (Newbury)
Essex Street,
off Andover Road (A343),
Near Newbury
Tel: 01635-47658

Finchampstead CC
Finchampstead Park,
Reading
Tel: 0118-973-2890

Kidmore End CC
Gallowstree Common,
Kidmore End, Nr Reading
Tel: 0118-9724143

Hungerford CC
Recreation Ground, Hungerford
Tel: 01488-682663

Hurst CC
Wokingham Road,
Hurst, Reading
Tel: 0118-934-0088

Reading CC
Sonning Lane,
Reading
Tel: 0118-699049

Buckinghamshire CCC

Amersham CC
Shardeloes, Amersham Old Town
Tel: 01494-433020

Ascott Park
Ascott Park,
Wing
Tel: 01296-688942

Aylesbury Town CC
Wendover Road, Aylesbury
Tel: 01296-415187

Beaconsfield CC
Wilton Park, Oxford Road
Beaconsfield Old Town
(London side of town on A40)
Tel: 01494-674134

High Wycombe CC
London Road,
High Wycombe
Tel: 01494-522611

Marlow CC
Pound Lane, High Street,
Marlow
Tel: 016284-83638

Milton Keynes
Campbell Park,
Central Milton Keynes
Tel: 01908-233600
(See page 118)

Slough CC
Chalvey Road, Slough
Tel: 01753-520982

Wormsley
Wormsley Estate,
Nr. Stokenchurch
Tel : 01494-484443 / 484449

Cambridgeshire CCC

Fenner's
(Cambridge University Ground)
Mortimer Road, Cambridge
Tel: 01223-353552
(See page 98)

March CC
The Avenue Sports Ground,
Burrowmoor Road, March
Tel: 01354-652029

Saffron Walden CC
Anglo American Park,
Saffron Waldron, Essex
Tel: 01799-522683

Wisbech CC
Harecroft Road,
Wisbech
Tel: 01945-585429

Cheshire CCC

Alderley Edge CC
Moss Lane,
Alderley Edge
Tel: 01625-584733

Boughton Hall CC,
Boughton Hall Avenue,
Filkins Lane, Chester
Tel: 01244-326072

125

Bowdon CC
South Downs Rd, Bowdon
Tel: 0161-928-1358

Nantwich CC
Whitehouse Lane, Nantwich
Tel: 01270-626155

Neston CC
Parkgate, South Wirral
Tel: 0151-336-4199

New Brighton CC
Rake Lane, Wallasey
Tel: 0151-639-4900

Oxton CC
Townfield Lane,
Birkenhead
Tel: 0151-652-1331

Toft CC
Chelford Road, Knutsford
Tel: 01565-632734

Warrington CC
Walton Lea Road,
Higher Walton
Warrington
Tel: 01925-263210

Cornwall CCC

Camborne CC
Roskear, Camborne
Tel: 01209-715478

Falmouth CC
Trescobeas, Falmouth
Tel: 01326-374000

Helston CC
Beacon Park,
Clodgey Lane, Helston
Tel: 01326-573423

Penzance CC
St Clare Ground,
St Clare Street, Penzance
Tel: 01736-362960

St Austell CC
Wheal Eliza, Bethel
St Austell
Tel: 01726-72588

Truro CC
Boscawen Park, Truro
Tel: 01872-277468

Cumberland CCC

Askam CC
James Street, Askam,
Cumbria
Tel: 01229-464576

Barrow CC
Abbey Road, Barrow, Cumbria
Tel: 01229-825201

Carlisle CC
Edenside, Carlisle, Cumbria
Tel: 01228-28593

Millom CC
St George's Road, Millom, Cumbria
Tel: 01229-772839

Netherfield CC
Parkside Road, Kendal,
Cumbria
Tel: 01539-724051

Penrith CC
Tynefield Park, Penrith,
Cumbria
Tel: 01768-863087

Devon CCC

Bovey Tracey CC
The Recreation Ground
Newton Road,
Bovey Tracey
Tel: 01626-832061

Budleigh Salterton CC
Ottermouth,
Budleigh Salterton
Tel: 01395-446269

Exmouth CC
The Maer Ground,
The Sea Front,
Exmouth
Tel: 01395-272771

North Devon CC
Sandhills,
Instow
Tel: 01271-860663

Sidmouth CC
Fortfield Terrace,
Sidmouth
Tel: 01395-513229

Torquay CC
Recreation Ground,
The Sea Front, Torquay
Tel: 01803-292001

United Services CC
Mount Wise,
Plymouth
Tel: 01752-563777 (Ex 3548)

Dorset CCC

Bournemouth CC
Dean Park,
Cavendish Road,
Bournemouth
Tel: 01202-295206

Dorchester CC
The Recreation Ground
Dorchester
Tel: 01305-263641

Sherborne School
Horsecastle, Sherborne
Tel: 01935-812431

Weymouth CC
Redlands Sports Ground
Dorchester Road,
Weymouth
Tel: 01305-813113

Herefordshire CCC

Brockhampton CC
The Park,
Brockhampton
Tel: None

Colwall CC
Stowe Lane, Colwall
Tel: 01684-541050

Dales CC
Mill Street, Leominster
Tel: None

Hereford City CC
Grandstand Road,
Hereford
Tel: 01432-273098

Kington CC
Recreation Ground
Kington
Tel: 01544-230095

Luctonians CC
Kingsland
Nr- Leominster
Tel: 01568-708345

Hertfordshire CCC

Bishop's Stortford CC
Cricketfield Lane,
Bishop's Stortford
Tel: 01279-654463

Hertford CC
Balls Park,
Mangrove Road, Hertford
Tel: 01992-581983

Hitchin CC
Lucas Lane,
Hitchin
Tel: 01462-434468

Long Marston CC
Cheddington,
Long Marston
Tel: 01296-661706

Radlett CC
Cobden Hill,
Watling Street,
Radlett
Tel: 01923-856348

St Albans CC
Clarence Park Road, St Albans
Tel: 01727-850388

Shenley Cricket Centre
(The Denis Compton Ground)
Radlett Lane, Shenley
Tel: 01923-859022
(See page 121)

Stevenage CC
Ditchmore Lane,
Stevenage Old Town
Tel: 01483-351075

Tring Park CC
Station Road,
Tring
Tel : 01442-823080

Lincolnshire CCC

Bourne CC
Abbey Lawn, Bourne
Tel: 01778-423641

Cleethorpes CC
Chichester Road, Cleethorpes
Tel: 01472-691271
(See page 118)

Grantham CC
Gorse Lane, Grantham
Tel: 01476-563742

Grimsby Town CC
Augusta Street,
Grimsby
Tel: 01472-360357

Lincoln Lindum C.C.
St Giles Avenue, Wragby Road,
Lincoln
Tel: 01522-526592

Sleaford CC
London Road,
Sleaford
Tel: 01529-303368

Norfolk CCC

Lakenham Cricket Ground
Lakenham Sports & Leisure Centre
Cricket Ground Road, Norwich
Tel: 01603-477477

North Runcton CC
North Runcton
Near Kings Lynn
Tel: None

Northumberland CCC

County Cricket Ground
Osborne Avenue,
Jesmond, Newcastle on Tyne
Tel: 0191-281-2738 / 0775

Tynemouth CC
Preston Avenue
North Shields
Tel: 0191-257-6865

Oxfordshire CCC

Aston Rowant CC
Butts Way, Kingston Blount,
Oxfordshire
Tel: None

Banbury CC
White Post Road,
Bodicote, Banbury
Tel: 01295-264368

Challow and Childrey CC
Vicarage Hill, East Challow,
Near Wantage
Tel: 01235-763335

Christ Church, Oxford
Iffley Road,
Oxford
Tel: 01865-243992

Rover Cowley
Roman Way Sports Ground,
Off Horspath Road,
Cowley,
Oxford
Tel: 01865-746152

Shipton-under-Wychwood CC
High Street,
Shipton-under-Wychwood
Tel: 01993-831337

Thame CC
Church Meadow, Church Road,
Thame
Tel: 01844-217799

Whitchurch CC
Heath Road
Whitchurch
Tel: 01948-663923

Shropshire CCC

Staffordshire CCC

Bridgnorth CC
Victoria Road,
High Town, Bridgnorth
Tel: 01746-764919

Brewood CC
Deansfield, Four Ashes Rd,
Brewood
Tel: 01902-850395

Newport CC
Audley Avenue,
Newport
Tel: 01952-810403

Cannock CC
The Morris Ground,
Four Crosses,
Hatherton, Cannock
Tel: 01543-502424/570348

Oswestry CC
Morda Road, Oswestry
Tel: 01691-653006

Dunstall CC
Deer Park, Dunstall
Tel: None

St George's CC
Church Road, St George's,
Telford
Tel: 01952-612911

Leek CC
Highfields, Ashbourne Road,
Leek
Tel: 01538-383693

Shifnal CC
Priorslee Road, Shifnal
Tel: 01952-462033

Longton CC
Trentham Road,
Blurton, Stoke on Trent
Tel: 01782-312278

Shrewsbury CC
London Road,
Shrewsbury
Tel: 01743-363655

Stone CC
Lichfield Road, Stone
Tel: 01785-813068

Wellington CC
Orleton Park,
Wellington
Tel: 01952-251539

Walsall CC
The Gorway,
Gorway Road, Walsall
Tel: 01922-22094

Suffolk CCC

Bury St Edmunds CC
The Victory Ground,
Nowton Road,
Bury St Edmunds
Tel: 01284-754592

Copdock & Old Ipswichians CC
Old London Road
Copdock
Tel: 01473-730752

Exning CC
Exning Village
Tel: None

Framlingham College
Woodbridge,
Framlingham
Tel: None

Ipswich School
Ivry Street,
Ipswich
Tel: 01473-214933

Mildenhall CC
Wamil Way,
Mildenhall
Tel: 01638-712018

Ransomes / Reavell Sports Club
Sidegate Avenue,
Ipswich
Tel: 01473-726134

Wales (Minor Counties) CCC

Abergavenny CC
Avenue Road,
Abergavenny
Tel: 01823-852350
(See page 111)

Colwyn Bay CC
Penryhn Avenue,
Rhos-on-Sea, Colwyn Bay
Tel: 01492-544103
(See page 112)

Newport CC
Spytty Park,
Newport
Tel: 01633-281236

Northop Hall CC
Smythy Lane,
Northop Hall,
Near Mold, North Wales
Tel: 01244-810461

Panteg CC, (Newport)
Panteg, Near Newport, Gwent
Tel: 01495-756117 or
01495-755468

Penarth CC
Athletic Ground, Lavernock Road,
Penarth, South Glamorgan
Tel: 01222-708402

Pontarddulais CC
Flosyrefail Ground,
Pontarddulais, West Glamorgan
Tel: 01792-882256

131

Pontypridd CC
Ynysangharad Park, Pontypridd
Tel: 01443-404699 (park)
or 490155 (clubhouse)
(See page 112)

St Fagans CC
St Fagans, Near Cardiff
Tel: 01222-566591

Swansea CC
St Helens Ground
Swansea
Tel: 01792-424242
(See page 112)

Ynsygerwn CC
Main Road,
Aberdulais
Tel: 01639-642547

Wiltshire CCC

Corsham CC
Station Road,
Corsham
Tel: 01249-713929

Marlborough CC
Savernake Forest,
Marlborough,
Tel: None

South Wilts CC
Bemerton Sports Ground,
Wilton Road, Salisbury
Tel: 01722-327108

Swindon CC
The County Ground,
Swindon
Tel: 01793-523088

Warminster CC
Samboume Road, Warminster
Tel: 01985-219039

Trowbridge CC
County Ground, Timbrell Street,
Trowbridge
Tel: 01225-752538

Westbury CC
Leighton Sports Ground,
Wellhead Lane, Westbury
Tel: 01373-826438

County E-MAIL and WEB SITES

MC
Du **MCC/ECB** Web: lords.org   email: ecb.co.uk   org.uk
Glɛ **Durham** Web: durham-ccc.org.uk   email: marketing@durham-ccc.org.uk
Ha **Glamorgan** Web: glamorgan.cricket.org email: glam@ecb.co.uk   .co.uk
Ke **Hampshire** Web: hampshire.cricket.org email: enquiries.hants@ecb.co.uk   uk
Laı **Kent** email: kent-cricket@msn.com   ;n.com
No **Lancashire** Web: lccc.co.uk
Suı **Nottinghamshire** Web: trentbridge.co.uk
Wɛ **Surrey** Web: surreyccc.co.uk
Yorkshire **Warwickshire** Web: warwickccc.org.uk email: info@warwickccc.org.uk
     Yorkshire Web: yorkshireccc.org.uk   email: cricket@yorkshireccc.org.uk   rg.uk

Yorkshire   *web*   yorkshıreccc.org.uk e-*mau* crıckeı@yorksnıreccc.org.u

Quiz answers

1. Glamorgan vs. Cambridge University June 1963
2. 29.5.1963.Manchester – Flavell (Lancashire v Worcester) 1932 Sheffield – Fisher (Yorkshire v Somerset).
3. *Grace* – 318 in 1896 against Yorkshire.
Townsend – 214 in 1906 against Worcestershire.
Hammond – 231 in 1933 against Derbyshire.
Zaheer Abbas – 205 in 1977 against Sussex.
Shaun Young - 237 in 1997 against Derbyshire.
4. Field Marshal Lord Montgomery
5. Leyton – Essex v Somerset
6. Neath
7. Old Trafford
8. Canterbury
9. Cheltenham – Gloucestershire v Somerset 1893 (stumped Brain b Townsend)
11. Taunton
12. St John's, Antigua
13. Derbyshire
14. Northampton 1920
15. Wellington
16. Southend
17. Canterbury
18. John Snow   Hastings July 1.
19. Torquay – August 24 1969.
20. Glamorgan.
21. Queens Park, Chesterfield.
22. Colchester.
23. Sabina Park.
24. Frome.
25. Abergavenny.
26. Basingstoke.
27. Eleven maids of Bramley and eleven maids of Hambleton.
28. William Clarke.
29. Yorkshire : Middlesborough.
30. Headingley 1932.
31. Melbourne 1877.
32. Old Trafford – 1900.
33. Dover August 1937.
34. Sir Arthur Conan Doyle.
35. United Services Ground – Portsmouth.
36. Gloucestershire.
37. St. Helens's, Swansea.
38. Severn (New Road); Tone (Taunton); Taff (Sophia Gardens); Can (Chelmsford); Avon (Bath).
39. Southgate.
40. Derbyshire, Warwickshire, Leicestershire and Yorkshire.
41. Southend, Maidstone and Neath
42. New Road; Sophia Gardens; The Oval; Canterbury and Headingley.
43. Northampton - Surrey vs. Northampton 1957
44. Brisbane - Australia vs. West Indies 1960-61.
45. Blackheath; Dover; Gravesend; Tonbridge.
46. Hastings.
47. Lord's
48. Georgetown, Guyana.
49. Old Trafford
50. Delhi.

More Books from London League Publications

From Arundel to Zimbabwe
A Cricket Followers' Guide to British
and International Cricket Grounds

Our first cricket grounds guide. The
detailed information includes all
international test and county grounds.
Essential if having a cricket holiday in
another country. Over 30 photos, local
maps and descriptions of grounds.
**Published in April 1997. Original price
£6.50.**
Special offer to readers of this book:
£3.00 including postage

From
ARUNDEL
to
ZIMBABWE

A Cricket
Followers' Guide
to British and
International Cricket
Grounds

by Robin Osmond, Peter David Lush and Dave Farrar

Boxing Shadows	*Tries in the Valleys*
1,500 Boxing Quiz Questions	**A History of Rugby League in Wales**
By Ralph Oates	All internationals and clubs covered.
	Interviews with key people. Many photos.
Published price £6.95	Published April 1998 at £14.95.
Now £4.00 post free	**Special offer £12.00 post free**

To order any of the above books, make cheques payable to:
London League Publications Ltd. No credit cards.
Send to:
London League Publications Ltd, PO Box 10441, London E14 0SB.
All books post free.

If you have an idea for a book or comments on any LLP publications
Please contact us at the above address, telephone / fax on 0171-515-2001
or E-Mail us at cdfarrar@compuserve.com.
We look forward to hearing from you.